TRANSACTIONAL ANALYSIS IN ORGANISATIONS

BY

KERI PHILLIPS

Published by: Keri Phillips Associates

112 Woodstock Court
Tatton Road
Handforth
Cheshire SK9 3SE
United Kingdom

+44(0) 1625 520124

ISBN: 0-9519991-1-7

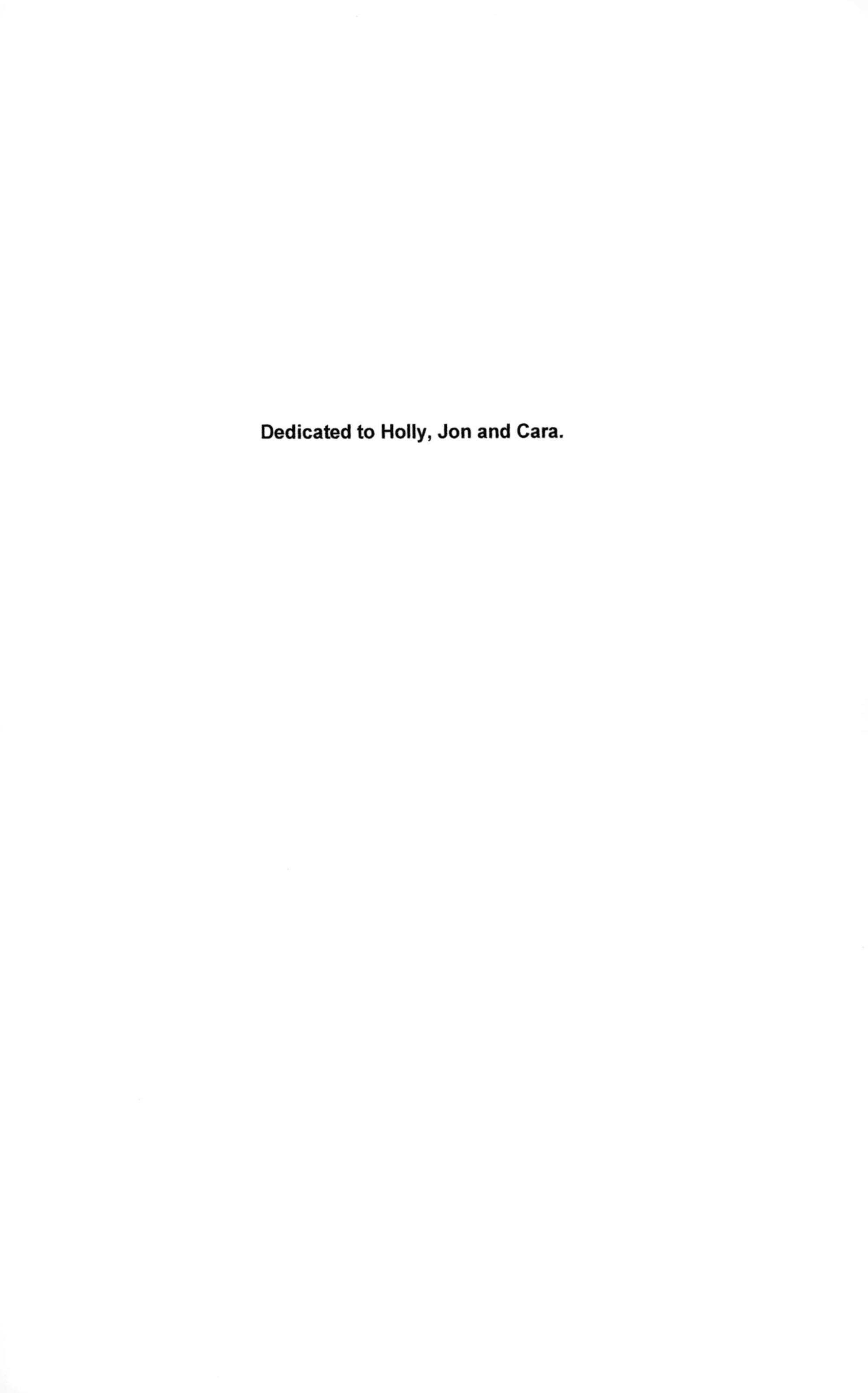

Dedicated to Holly, Jon and Cara.

CONTENTS

LIST OF FIGURES

PREFACE

It is more than thirty years since I first began to learn about Transactional Analysis. I vividly remember my delight and excitement as childhood and family experiences suddenly began to fall into place, these insights accompanied by an almost audible, 'Now I can see why I'm like I am !' Then there was all that delightful theory to get my teeth into. I am sure I must have driven many people crazy as I tried to psychoanalyse them.

I like to think that after that initial infatuation my love affair then matured a little, particularly as I took some professional training and received excellent supervision. At that time TA was hugely popular in the world of management development and I particularly remember the great pleasure I took in running TA for trainers courses, designed for internal trainers and consultants.

Over the years the theory and practice of TA has evolved, as have the professional institutions, conferences and workshops which are integral to its development. New generations of learners arrive and in many ways it is for them that I write. Yet I must also acknowledge my own self interest, namely that in the writing I can revisit and sometime relive treasured moments from this long romance.

This booklet has been written for managers, consultants and trainers who want an accessible summary of the main features of TA, together with an indication of how it might be applied in management and organisation development. It is intended to be an introductory publication.

The first part covers the key points of theory, the second part looks at some of the possible uses and challenges in using TA in an organisational setting. Finally, there are some references and contacts for further reading, training and development.

I should like to acknowledge my debt to Dave Barker, a teacher who became a colleague and a friend.

Whether, dear reader, you are simply flirting or looking for something a little more serious, you are most welcome.

Keri Phillips.

Keri5@btopenworld.com

INTRODUCTION

Eric Berne (1910-1970), the originator of Transactional Analysis (TA), trained as a psychiatrist and psychoanalyst and was keen to develop methods of treatment which were simple yet effective. One could argue that 'profound simplicity' was his mantra, and this typifies the best practice of TA today; a deceptively simple model which has the potential to generate deep, sometimes unsettling and delightful, insights. One of Berne's fundamental values was respect; he wanted to have an approach which meant that he could work with clients in a truly open and collaborative way. Also, as part of the humanistic tradition, he made the following assumptions: people have, at their core, a positive intent; sometimes people need to rediscover their true purpose; people live their lives on the basis of aware or unaware decisions; and what has been decided can be re-decided.

TA is a theory of personality, behaviour and communication. As such, it provides a framework for understanding what might be going on 'inside somebody', how this links to what they are actually seen to do and the consequences, 'positive' or 'negative' for their relationship with others. Most TA practitioners would accept that at its best TA can only provide an imperfect snapshot of a human being, with all her or his strengths, frailties, ambitions, clarity and confusions.

What follows are brief descriptions of most of the major facets of TA theory. Berne did not develop them all, however, it is fair to say that he anticipated many of the developments which took place after his death. The theory is sufficiently rich that it is possible to concentrate only on one or two aspects when helping clients. It is not an 'all or nothing' model.

TA THEORY

As already mentioned, one of Berne's beliefs was the importance of respect; respect for self and others. A TA model which captures this and was popularised by Thomas Harris is **life positions**[1]. This identifies the ways in which a person can relate to self and others at particular point in time. There are four basic life positions as shown here (Fig 1):

Figure 1: Life Positions

I'm not OK – You're OK (I– U+)	I'm OK – You're OK (I+ U+)
I'm not OK – You're not OK (I– U–)	I'm OK – You're not OK (I+ U–)

The I+U+ life position, sometimes known as the 'get on with' position[2], is where the person does not put self or others down and deals with concerns openly and honestly. Praise and criticism are given, problems are dealt with as constructively as possible, grudges are not held and the person's energy is directed towards learning.

The I+U- life position, sometimes known as the 'get rid of ' position, is where the person sees himself or herself as superior in some way. They will see others as pathetic, inferior, incompetent and untrustworthy and therefore deserving of contempt, condescension or anger.

The I-U+ life position, sometimes known as the 'get away from' position, is where the person 'puts self down', regarding others as more clever, more attractive, more successful or somehow better. Common feelings would be inadequacy, powerlessness, inferiority and regret.

The I-U- life position, sometimes known as the 'get nowhere position', is where the person has no respect for self or others. He or she sees self and the world as unchangeable, and will often feel confused and aimless.

There can be many variations contained within this model. First, feelings may vary greatly in intensity. For example, in the I-U+ position one person may simply feel a bit 'one down', that in some vague way other people seem just that bit luckier. From that same position somebody else might have much more intense feelings, filled with deep envy and resentment.

Secondly, there may be great differences in the frequency with which a person 'visits' a particular life position. Arguably, each of us during a normal working day may have experience of all four. However there may well be people who live their lives from predominantly just one position. From these positions certain attitudes, beliefs and behaviours will flow, as elaborated in other aspects of TA theory.

Berne's central idea of **ego states** was developed from his early work on intuition[3]. It proposes the classification of personality into three 'sub-personalities', or 'ego-states', each with characteristic attitudes, feelings, behaviour and language. The three basic ego states are referred to as the Parent, Adult and Child. Typically, this is shown as the following (Fig 2):

Figure 2: Ego States

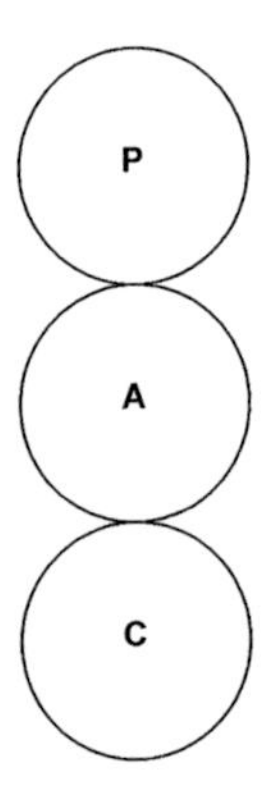

The Parent (taught concept of life) is drawn from the various 'authority figures' that we experience in our lives. This will frequently be the mother or father, but not necessarily so. For example a grandmother might be much more influential then a frequently absent father. Our Parent ego state may be added to at any stage of our lives. We might, for example, be particularly influenced at the age of thirty five by a charismatic boss, and we want very much to be like her. So if ever we behave like one of these 'parent figures' did, then we are using our Parent ego state. Clearly this could cover many features. However, generally the Parent - sets limits, disciplines, judges, criticises, gives advice and guidance, protects and nurtures, keeps traditions, makes and enforces rules about how life should be. These rules might range from 'eat your greens and clean your shoes', to 'do well at school', 'never challenge me', 'life is about fun'...... All these components, big and small, make up the Parent ego state.

The Adult (the thought concept of life) is that part of us which works things out by gathering facts, generating options and making decisions based on that evidence. It can appear quite unemotional and will often pride itself, justifiably or not, on being objective. The associated ability to conceptualise is very much an Adult function. However, it does not mean 'mature.' Quite often the Adult mediates the 'shoulds' of the Parent, the 'wants' of the Child in relation to the resources and demands of the world; 'I think I've got better things to do than clean my shoes every day.'

The Child (the felt concept of life) consists of a mosaic of childhood experiences and feelings from birth (some would even say pre-birth) to late adolescence. As such some of the experiences will be preverbal and lodged deep in our body and soul. Others will be more accessible. Clearly, such experiences may be nourishing, loving and life enhancing, or destructive and limiting or a mixture. As a grown up man or woman I may feel at times as I did when seven months, seven years or seventeen years old.

The Child ego state may be fun loving, energetic, compliant, polite, creative and rebellious.

As already mentioned, the 'raw material' of the ego states will be infinite in its variety and intensity. However, Berne sought to make some rough generalisations about what the content might be. He consequently broke the Parent and Child ego states into facets.

The Parent, he described as having a Nurturing and Critical aspects.

The Nurturing Parent takes care of, and looks after, self and others. When doing this appropriately, and from an I+ U+ position, then this is typified as the positive Nurturing Parent (+NP). If used to excess or inappropriately then it is seen as smothering. This is then regarded as the negative Nurturing Parent (–NP).

The Critical Parent sets limits, disciplines, judges and criticises self and others. Once again, if this takes place from an I+U+ position, namely with respect, then this is seen as the positive Critical Parent (+CP). If used to excess or inappropriately then it is seen as oppressive. This is then regarded as the negative Critical Parent (–CP).

The Child, he described as having a Free/Natural aspect and an Adapted aspect.

The Free Child is spontaneous, adventurous, joyful, angry, sad, and fun loving. When this happens in a way that is damaging neither for self nor others (I+ U+) then this is seen as positive Free Child (+FC). If acting inappropriately, for example, obsessed with own needs, then this would be regarded as the negative Free Child (–FC).

The Adapted Child is motivated by the need to get along with authority figures or to get attention from them. It may therefore be compliant, or rebellious or both. This may happen in a positive way, for example, conforming to the hygiene rules when visiting a friend in hospital; this would be the positive Adapted Child (+AC). If this aspect is overly concerned to comply - always wanting to please everybody all the time - or is overly rebellious - always saying no, regardless of the other person's case, then this is regarded as negative Adapted Child (–AC). It is interesting to note that rebellion and compliance are regarded as two sides of the same coin and that a person may suddenly switch from one to the other. For example, years of loyal service followed by 'out of character' outrageous behaviour. Or the person who is taken advantage of because he is always willing to accept more work, and then he suddenly one day has a furious outburst and storms out of the office. Everyone is shocked, 'I can't imagine what's got into Joe today!'

The Child ego state is sometimes regarded as having a third aspect, known as the 'Little Professor' (LP). This is the intuitive and creative part which understands things and people in a way which is different from Adult logic. The Little Professor not only has flashes of inspiration, but can be adept at knowing how to get through to people, for good or ill. It is often regarded as a 'trigger' for the other ego states.

Berne did not divide the Adult into facets, but some would also regard this ego state as having a negative side, for example excessive clinical detachment (–A); a member of staff starts crying in the office because his partner has left him, and his boss takes him to one side and says,' What options do you have...?'

The summarising diagrams are shown below Fig 3):

Figure 3: Facets of the Ego States

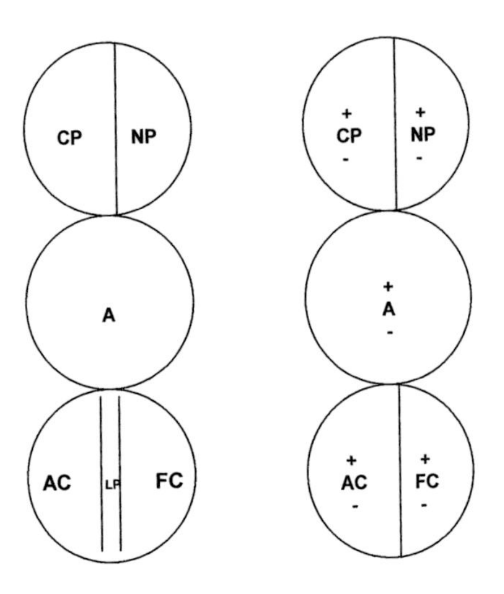

Some further examples of the typical words, behaviours and attitudes for the various facets of the ego states are given below (Fig 4):

Figure 4: Typical Features of the Ego States

	Words	Behaviours	Attitudes
Critical Parent	You must always …… Make sure you …. How could you be so stupid as to …. It's dangerous to …. We've got certain standards round here	Pointing finger Hands on hips Looking down on Steepled fingers	Patronising Condescending Judgemental Concerned Strict Disgusted
Nurturing Parent	I'll take care of it for you Wrap up warm Don't worry, better luck next time Well Done!	Pat on the back	Comforting Making excuses/ allowances Suffocating
Adult	What? Why? When? How? Is it practical? What is the logic?	Open Thoughtful Precise	Interested Detached Evaluative
Adapted Child	Please let me I won't ! Why me again?	Crestfallen Slumped Vigorous head nodding Chin forward	Whiny Placating Defiant
Free Child	I want! Sounds great! That's exciting!	Laughing with Noisy crying Energetic	Spontaneous Relaxed Changeable

In an 'ideal world', energy would flow freely amongst and between all the positive aspects of all the ego states. However, frequently this is not the case. The person may consciously or unconsciously exclude the use of certain ego states. She might habitually tend to react to the world in a Critical Parent way. For example if something goes wrong, she always looks for something or someone to blame. The technical term for this is '**exclusion**', and is generally shown as below (Fig 5):

Figure 5: Exclusion

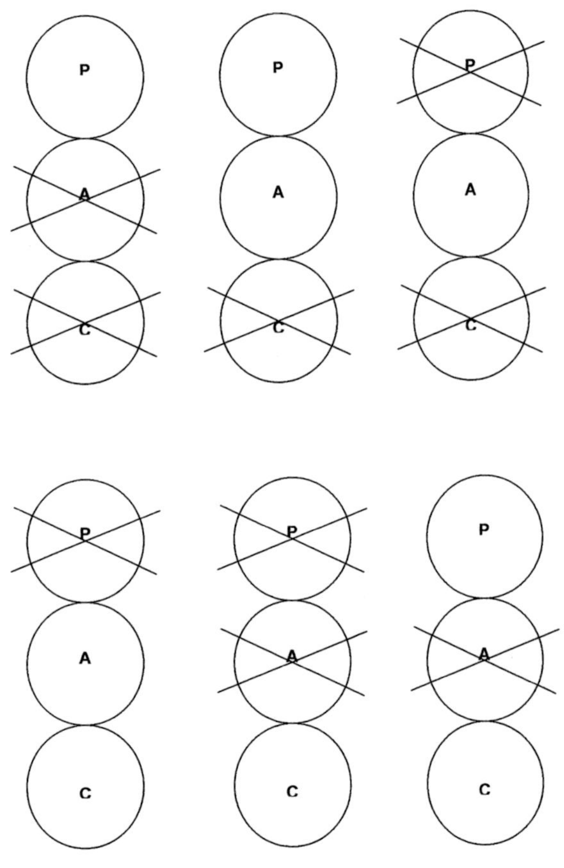

Exclusion can be the result of a variety of experiences, often originating in childhood:

- Certain behaviours being rewarded. For example, the elder sister always gets a lot of praise from Mum for looking after her little brother. She might learn to ignore her own Free Child needs and carry this behaviour into later life, perhaps as a partner or manager. Equally she might grow up into a narcissist in order to make up for lost time.

- Certain behaviours being punished. For example, the younger brother who gets used to being pampered and is cold shouldered if he starts being too independent. He might become a man with a strong need to be mothered. Equally he might grow up into an obsessively self reliant adult who would rather suffer than ask for help.

- Certain behaviours are 'modelled' by the parents. For example, the mother provides a living case study of long suffering regret and the daughter 'decides', "OK so that's what marriage is all about." Anything is then possible between the extremes rushing into marriage as a demonstration of dutiful solidarity; or long held and deep resistance to marriage even to somebody who is, by general consensus, 'ideal'.

When people with exclusions come together then sometimes this leads to **symbiosis**. Unlike the use of the word in the animal kingdom, this is often seen in TA as being mutually unhelpful. It means, two people acting as if between them they had one full set of ego states. One example is below (Fig 6):

Figure 6: Symbiosis

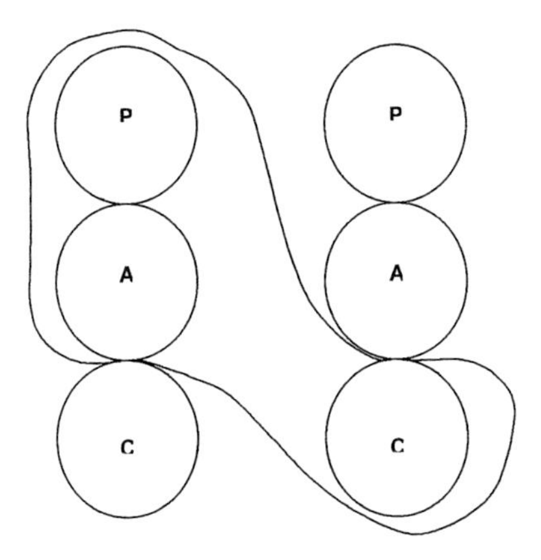

Here one person is always the 'responsible one', looking after and making decisions, but never allows herself to have her own needs. By contrast, the other one is always the 'needy one', and does not allow himself to develop his problem solving (A), or controlling (CP), or nurturing (NP) capabilities. Sometimes people can get into a habit and lock themselves a variety of symbiotic relationships; always the carer with mum, the problem solver with a younger sister and whiny child with a friend. At work, it might be seen when there is a member of staff who always likes to be the joker at team meetings, but then always takes it too far and has to be told off by his boss.

There can also be **competitive symbiosis**. One of its more frequent illustrations would be where two partners arrive home from work totally exhausted. Essentially each wants to be looked after, but neither is explicit about this and the evening is spent in an atmosphere of random irritability punctuated by the sound of clattering saucepans in the kitchen.

Sometimes the boundaries between the ego states are not clear and '**contamination**' can occur. If the Child contaminates the Adult then fantasies are regarded as facts. 'We all know that the MD wants to destroy us!' If the Parent contaminates the Adult then prejudices are treated as facts. 'Those in R&D are always incapable of feeling anything; they're useless to work with'. The 'horns and halo effect' is also an example of contamination. 'He's wearing the right school tie, he must be a good candidate'. Sometimes the person's 'investment' in the contamination is so great that he literally does not see evidence to the contrary. This will be particularly likely if others respond with similar contaminations. For example, a beleaguered team might always perceive an offer of help with suspicion and reject it. Contamination is generally shown as in the diagram below (Fig 7):

Figure 7: Contamination

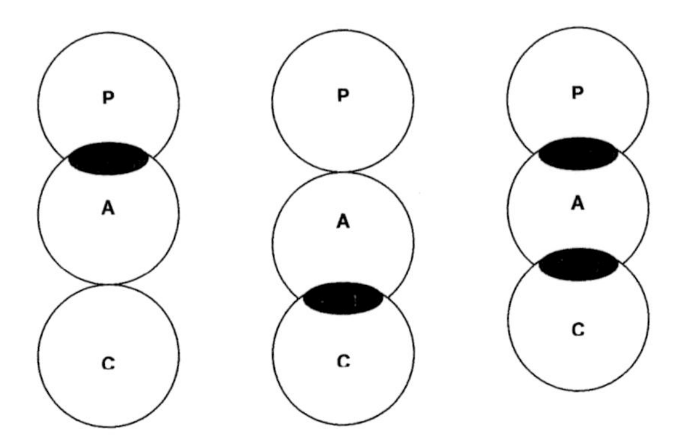

The greater the overlap of the circles, the greater the extent of the contamination. In the world of therapy, diagnosis might on occasion extend to the point where the patient is seen as having an overlap between both Parent and Child. In other words, the Adult is scarcely free at all from contamination.

Transactions describes what can happen between people when they communicate.

With **complementary transactions** the person initiating the communication gets the response for which he was looking. The following examples illustrate this (Fig 8):

Figure 8: Complementary Transactions

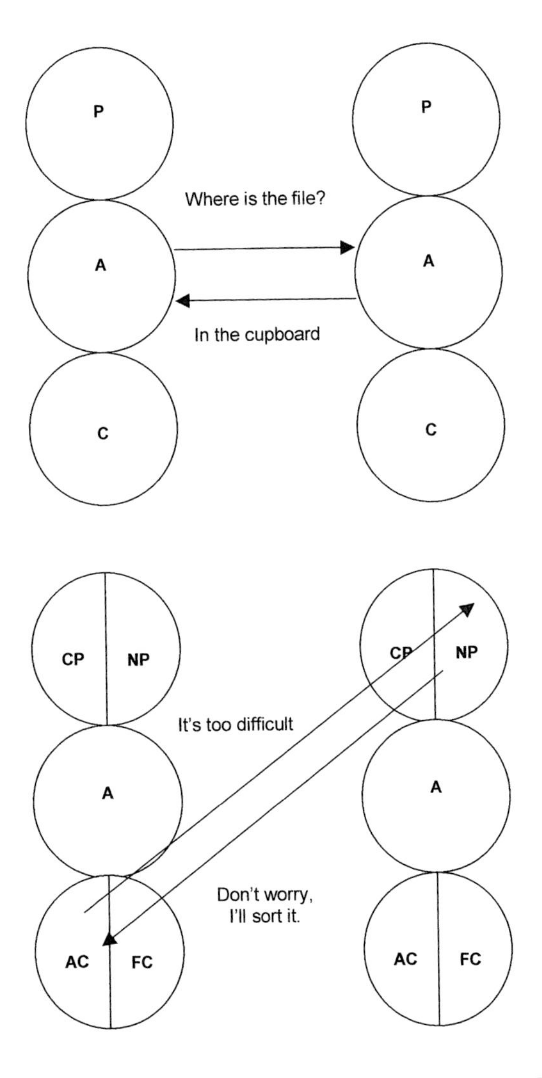

Complementary transactions have the potential to go on indefinitely since, superficially, each is responding to the other's need. However, as seen with symbiosis, this is not necessarily a 'healthy' relationship.

With **crossed transactions** there is an unexpected response. As can be seen from the example below (Fig 9) it is not necessarily a negative exchange. By crossing the transaction, the second person may be 'inviting' the other person to behave differently; for example to think for herself. This is obviously vital for managers who want to develop their staff. Incidentally, the use of the word 'invite' is particularly relevant since there is an underlying principle in TA that people cannot be forced to behave or feel in any particular way. There is always a choice about how to respond to others. By way of a side comment, it is interesting to note Shea Schiff's workshop contribution that when working with people who are quite agitated and disturbed then it can sometimes be very difficult not to begin absorbing some of their feelings, almost through osmosis.

Figure 9: Crossed Transactions

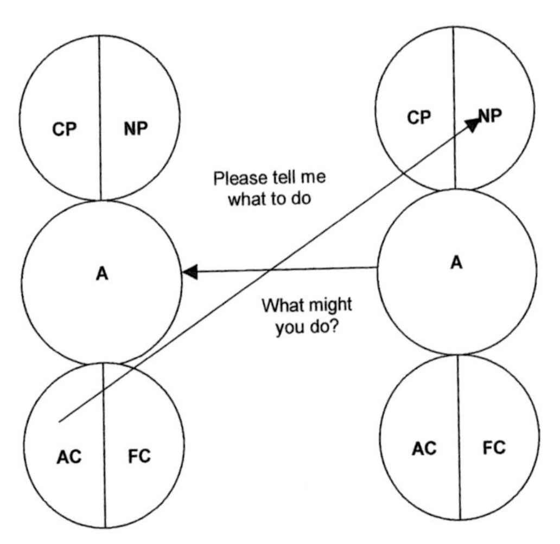

With **ulterior transactions** (Fig 10) the person communicates at two levels, social and psychological, at the same time. The psychological level will be conveyed non verbally, for example tone of voice and eye contact and, having the most emotional energy behind it, is likely to be key in determining the outcome of the communication.

Figure 10: Ulterior Transactions

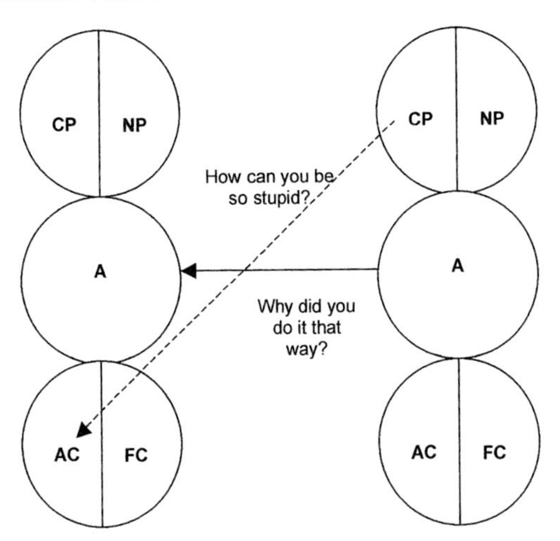

Once again, ulterior transactions are not by definition a 'bad thing'. For example, an offer of help can be particularly influential if it conveys some Parent support, some Adult options and some Child warmth. Such a communication may then tap into positive aspects in all the ego states of the other person. This is sometimes known as a **bull's eye transaction**. It has relevance to change management in organisations; see, for example, the later points on resistance to change in 'Applying TA in Organisations'.

The ego states will be involved not only with external but also internal communication. The **internal dialogue** describes one way this might happen. For example, I want to apply for an exciting new job but my internal Critical Parent tells me not to bother, saying I'll never be good enough (Fig 11). This is sometimes known as the **Parent tape**. In other words, an habitual replay of Parental rules or guidance in a way which may be stifling or oppressive.

Figure 11: Internal Dialogue

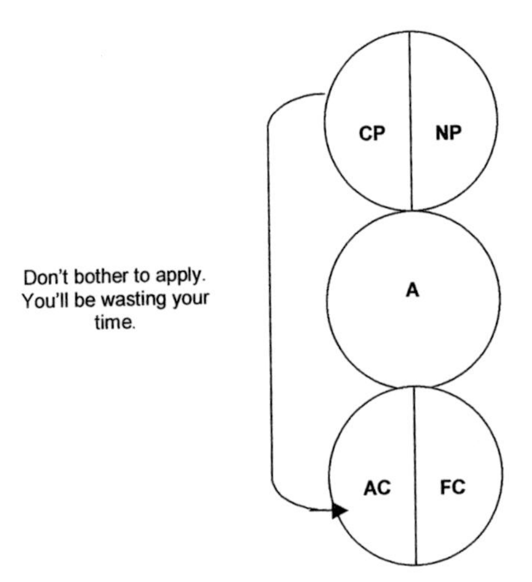

Often personal development is about changing the nature of the internal dialogue. For example, learning to turn the volume down on some of the stunting messages, replacing them perhaps with the positive Nurturing Parent; "have a go at applying for that job, I'm sure you will do well. If you don't get it there will surely be other opportunities."

With the internal dialogue, and transactions, **strokes** come into play. A basic concept in TA is that people want and need care, attention, love and recognition. This is probably most clearly the case with young children when, for example, they want to show off a pair of new shoes or put ice cream in the dvd player to get attention. Similarly, grown ups may try to get attention by working hard, pushing to be involved in a new project, sighing deeply ,buying a flashy new suit or sabotaging the photocopier. Just as people have choices about the way they seek recognition, so there are a number of ways in which recognition can be given (Fig 12):

Figure 12: Strokes

STROKE	VERBAL	NON VERBAL
Positive for Being	'I like you'	A smile
Positive for Doing	'Thank you for that report'	A performance bonus
Negative for Being	'You're a complete waste of space'	Not invited to a meeting
Negative for Doing	'As a result you will be downgraded'	Suddenly transferred to the Slough Office

A fundamental point is that negative strokes are preferable to no strokes at all, since at least some form of recognition is being offered. One famous example is the Hawthorne Experiments[4] (1924 – 1932) where people's job performance was maintained, despite declining working conditions, when the researchers were friendly and approachable. People may behave badly simply as a response to believing, rightly or wrongly, that they are being ignored. Beyond this generalisation, people's personality can vary greatly to the extent that they want and seek recognition. One person might be grateful to have her own office, somebody else might regard it as a punishment. There are clear links here to the notions of 'introversion' and 'extraversion' in the Myers Briggs Type Indicator[5]; the 'introvert' draws energy from time alone, the 'extravert' draws energy from being in the company of others.

One could argue that through upbringing each of us acquires a particular stroke pattern; namely, an expectation about the sort of strokes that will be given and received. These expectations may, realistically or otherwise, be carried forward into organisational life. We might then behave in ways to try and reproduce the stroking pattern which is familiar from childhood. This might reveal itself through **games**.

In many ways the idea of games popularised TA[6]. A game in TA is essentially a destructive way of spending time, involving the creation of situations for the exchange of negative strokes. This predictable outcome, or 'pay off', consists of 'bad' feelings for each player. A bad feeling is any feeling which occurs as a result of somebody putting themselves or somebody else down; for example, guilt, self righteousness, anger, depression or triumph. Games are learnt patterns of behaviour, often originating in childhood. They can vary in intensity from mild discomfort to physical harm. Game players intuitively, often even outside awareness, seek partners to play the complementary hand. The assumption is that for somebody to be successful in their put down, there has to be another player who lets herself be put down. It always takes a minimum of two people to play the TA game.

So, the clues to a game are: someone is being put down; there is an ulterior or hidden message; people feel 'bad'; both parties have a sense of 'here we go again'.

One of the most helpful and graphic ways of categorising games is through the **drama triangle**. This idea was formulated by Stephen Karpman[7] who analysed fairy stories, discovering that frequently three main roles were played out. He then identified ways in which these roles exist in everyday life. These are **Rescuer, Persecutor and Victim.**

The Rescuer has a life position of I+U– (–NP). He or she sees the world as a place filled with rather pathetic or helpless individuals who need to be protected from their own inadequacies and from Persecutors. Persecutors have the same life position as Rescuers, but they operate from negative Critical Parent. Consequently, they see the world as being full of pathetic individuals who need to be 'licked into shape'. Victims see themselves as unlucky individuals (–AC) who need to be taken care of, or controlled by others. In all this, the various parties need each other in order to maintain their view of the world and themselves. Again it is important to stress that much of this will be played outside awareness; a long established pattern, quite possibly originating in childhood, perhaps even absorbed with 'mother's milk'.

The usual way of portraying the interplay of these roles is shown as follows (Fig 13):

Figure 13: The Drama Triangle

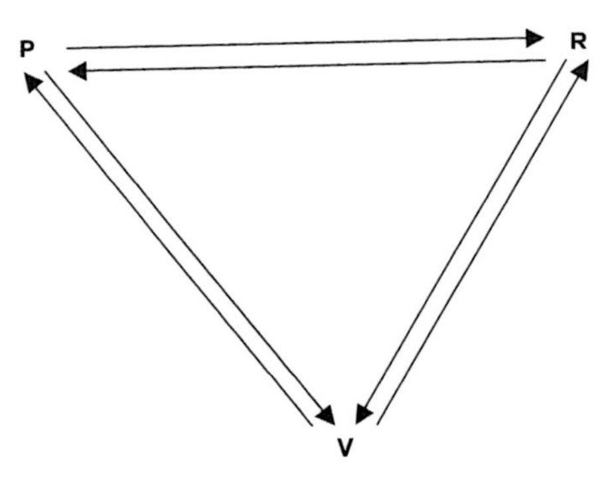

The arrows indicate that although somebody may have a favourite role, nevertheless they may well visit the other roles as well, particularly during the course of a game. For example, a member of staff (Victim) might frequently find reasons for underperforming, citing poor training, train delays, poor equipment and a sick pet rabbit. Each time he is able to persuade his boss (Rescuer) to give him one more chance. A really dedicated Rescuer might even bring into work a book called, 'A Layperson's Guide to Caring for Sick Rabbits'. Eventually the manager loses patience, exploding with anger, switching from Rescuer to Persecutor. He might even ask for his book back.

The staff member might then switch from Victim to Persecutor and take great delight in contacting the Personnel Department to complain that his boss has bullied him.

Some of the associated games are shown here (Fig 14):

Figure 14: Drama Triangle Games

Persecutor:

NIGYSOB (Now I've got you, you son of a bitch. The person who typically tries to put others down and score points off them).

Blemish (The person who *always* finds something wrong).

Corner (The person who verbally corners others).

Let's You And Him Fight (The person who sets up arguments between others).

If It Weren't For You (The person who blames others for their own unhappy life).

See What You Made Me Do (The person who will not accept responsibility for the mistakes they make).

Why Don't You..... Yes But..... (The person who can always find fault with somebody else's suggestions).

Rescuer:

I'm Only Trying To Help You (The person who keeps offering help – even when it s not needed – and is often upset when it is rejected).

What Would You Do Without Me? (The person who likes to think she is indispensable).

Happy To Help (The person who sees his sole purpose in life being to give help to others – even if they do not need it).

Victim:

Kick Me (The person who contrives to put herself down).

Why Does This Always Happen To Me? (The person who feels that he is always losing out).

Poor Me (The person who feels that life is always unfair to her).

Stupid (The person who pretends that he is too stupid to understand anything).

Do Me Something (The person who always expects others to solve his problems).

Harried (The person who is always in a hurry and feeling harassed).

It is sometimes said that, 'If you see yourself as a hammer then the world is full of nails.' The same principle applies to the Drama Triangle. The Rescuer, for example, has to 'see' Victim status in others in order to buttress her own view of herself. In extreme cases this is how little old ladies get taken across the road even when they did not want to go.

It is interesting to note that Steve Karpman sees each of the Drama Triangle roles as having '10% OKness': OK aggression in the Persecutor, OK caring in the Rescuer and OK vulnerability in the Victim. This is a useful reminder of the need for some compassion when using TA, recognising that it is important to distinguish between the person and their behaviour. Somebody behaving 'badly' is not by definition a 'bad' person. The decision, however, about whether to put them on the Christmas card list is a totally different matter.

Games are just one way of **time structuring** and exchanging strokes. Berne identified five others: **withdrawal**, which may be positive or negative; time alone to reflect and recharge batteries or an avoidance of others, based upon unhelpful, perhaps even destructive memories or assumptions. **Rituals** are tightly programmed exchanges where everybody knows what is going to happen next. If the ritual is broken it can be quite disconcerting. For example, one person says, 'How are you?', and the other person actually starts to tell him! **Pastimes** are transactions where both parties talk about a non threatening subject. They are not quite so predictable as rituals, but generally all know and accept the direction of the conversation: car talk, the weather, shopping, sport and so on. **Activities** are directed towards achieving a goal: writing a report, contributing to a meeting, organising finances. Activities may be productive and creative or a way of avoiding closeness with others; 'keeping busy'. **Intimacy** characterises those situations where the parties have a shared sense of trust, closeness, honesty and 'oneness.' This is very similar to the idea of 'contact' in gestalt[8]. It may come from a shared sense of achievement, working through conflict or sheer pleasure in enjoying each other's company. It is a rich source of positive strokes, engaging the Free

Child. Without opportunities for intimacy, a person may turn to other ways of structuring time, such as games, in order to exchange strokes.
Perhaps not surprisingly 'feelings' were an essential part of Berne's exposition. Indeed, a major contributor to TA theory, Claude Steiner, used the phrase 'emotional literacy'[9]; it has many parallels with emotional intelligence[10]. The aim for both Berne and Steiner was to help people understand their feelings, where they originated and which ones currently served any useful purpose. A fundamental theme in their writing was the assumption that frequently people experience in the 'here and now' feelings which are rooted in the recent or even distant past. Amongst the ideas developed by Berne to elaborate and explain this phenomenon was that of **stamps**.

The use of the word stamps came from trading stamps which has a slight similarity to loyalty cards. The issuing of trading stamps was a selling technique which is now much less in vogue. When buying a product the purchaser would be given a stamp which would be collected in books and then subsequently 'cashed in'. Somebody might, for example, cash in two books and be able to collect a 'free' frying pan. Alternatively he might collect twenty books and cash them in for a vacuum cleaner.

Berne drew parallels between this and the collecting of feelings which might subsequently be cashed in. One of the most obvious examples would be the person who has a difficult day at work, goes home and starts shouting at her partner for no obvious reason. An indication of the possible extremes might range from a mild air of irritability to an explosive and shocking outburst. The crucial point is that from the 'Martian point of view', a favourite phrase of Berne's meaning a totally objective observer, these feelings would have no obvious link to the present.

Berne suggested that people might vary not only in the stages at which they cashed in their stamps, but also the types of stamp they chose to collect: guilt, anger, depression, condescension. Essentially stamps are collected and stored in the negative Adapted Child, though their cashing in may be manifested by behaviour from any of the negative aspects of the ego states. Since the collecting takes place in the Child the person may not be aware of what she is doing. Indeed if challenged about it she may well, without any intended deception, claim that she had done nothing unusual or was in some way justified in her behaviour. So the aim of the 'helper', whether therapist, coach, counsellor or consultant, would be to help the client become aware of her stamp collections and the choices she had in dealing with them. Obviously, as described later in the section on coaching, there are questions of risk and appropriateness which arise here dependent on the helper's qualifications and contract with the client.

Two brief points to conclude this section on stamps; one is about vicarious stamp collecting. That is, collecting stamps on behalf of others. For example, inter-group conflict can sometimes be generated and maintained through this. 'How dare they say that to one of my team. I'm outraged. I'll get my own back!' Of course it does not have to be so technicolour as this; a low level, lingering resentment may equally be the result of ongoing indignation on behalf of others.

The second point is the idea of the 'hurt museum'. Namely, that a person might add substantially to her stamp collection by regularly revisiting a painful past experience. The 'exhibits' are regularly taken down and polished and indeed cherished as a justification for feeling 'bad' ; that is, angry , depressed, guilty and so on.

The other closely linked idea related to understanding feelings is that of **rackets**. A racket is a feeling which is inappropriate in:

Type - for example, somebody is cheated, but he feels guilty, instead of angry with the other person.

Intensity - for example, somebody missing out on promotion because of the boss's favouritism, feels 'slightly irritated'.

Duration - for example, somebody still gets furious about the teacher who, thirty years before, persuaded him to study engineering rather than his beloved art.

Rackets are learnt feelings (-AC) as opposed to 'real' feelings (+FC). They arise as a result the following:

The child being told what to feel. 'Don't get angry, it stops you looking pretty'

The child being rewarded or punished, through strokes, for having, or not having, certain types of feelings. For example, the child gets lots of attention for being cheerful and is ignored if appearing needy.

The child sees around her the feelings which are or are not an accepted 'currency'. For example she notices that her father gets sulky rather than angry; or that her mother only receives some tender loving care when she acts depressed.

The distinctions between racket and real feelings are summarised below (Fig 15):

Figure 15: Rackets and Real Feelings

RACKET FEELINGS	REAL (REACTIVE) FEELINGS
Adapted Child	Free Child
Learned as a way of getting strokes	Spontaneous without any particular aim
Often experienced by others as inauthentic, manipulative, or incongruent.	Usually experienced by others as genuine and appropriate
Tend to be habitual regardless of the circumstances.	One off and 'in the moment'

Once again it is important to remember that rackets, and the associated behaviours, are largely outside the person's awareness. They mostly originate in early childhood, become part of 'the way things are round here' and then continue to happen on 'automatic pilot'. So, taking the earlier example, the mother is not consciously contriving depression to get attention; it is simply a deeply ingrained habit in which she is likely genuinely to feel depressed. It is interesting to note that racket behaviour may well evoke racket behaviour in others leading for example, to collective depression.

All the elements of TA described above come into play with a person's **script**. A script is a 'life plan' which answers two fundamental questions: 'What sort of person am I?' and 'What happens to someone like me?' Scripts are multi-faceted : the raw material of childhood experiences is transformed into a storyline which has its own internal coherence dealing with such issues as closeness, work, parenthood, leadership, play, attractiveness, sexuality, vulnerability, cleverness........

All of an individual's games, strokes, contaminations, rackets, drama triangle positions and stamp collections support the script. A simplistic example: from my upbringing as a boy I might decide that my life's fulfilment would be to run a large and financially successful business. This might then allow me to avoid closeness by working all hours and by putting others down. I have then created a self-contained and self- fulfilling prophesy.

So far the negative aspects of scripts and scripting have been emphasised. Indeed, there is a strand of thought that scripts are by definition a bad thing since they deny an individual's autonomy. However it is perhaps more helpful, and paradoxically more liberating, to accept that there can be a huge range of different types of scripts. In terms of healthy individual development some of them may be largely positive, some largely negative and some a mixture. The aim of the helper would then be to increase the client's awareness of the negative or destructive elements in her script and to make some new decisions. For example, to help the business person find ways of maintaining financial success whilst getting closer to her children.

Most frequently, though not inevitably, it will be the child's parents who will be most influential in the creation of the script. Regarding this influence, wherever it originates, there are two particular aspects to mention here, illustrated below[11] (Fig 16):

Figure 16: Modified Script Matrix

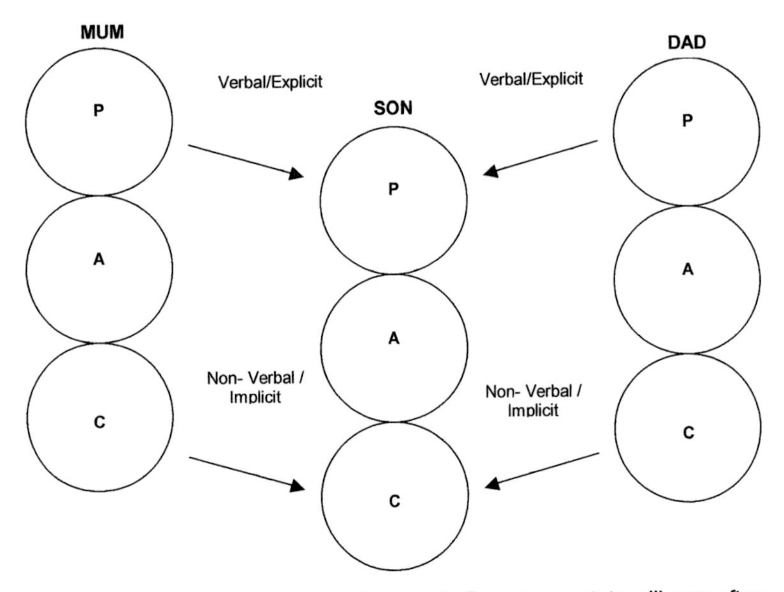

The scripting messages given from the carer's Parent ego state will very often be explicit and verbal; almost life's mottoes. 'Look for a safe and secure job, be adventurous and take risks, look after your money, pride comes before a fall....' There will be other messages that will be communicated from the carer's Child ego state. In contrast these will often be implicit and non verbal. The message, 'It's ok to get close to people' might simply be expressed through hugs, or 'if in doubt get angry', might be conveyed by a father who gets angry for no apparent reason. These latter, Child ego state messages are likely to be more powerful because they are expressed as a given, not open to discussion and with all the parent's own Child neediness behind it. This fundamental communication regarding the little boy or girl's identity, lovability and importance is conveyed non verbally in the early years of life, establishing the base of the script. As such it may well be outside the child's, and even the parent's conscious awareness. It may only be later in life that, for example, the grown up begins to realise that it's not a matter of life and death to work hard every hour that is available.

(Incidentally, this idea of being born into a family where there are implicit and explicit messages has parallels with joining an organisation. There will be the explicit rules, often described on induction courses. There will then be the implicit rules which emerge over time, perhaps conveyed by staff who help their new colleague understand 'how things are really done round here'.)

There will certainly be times when there are contradictions between the scripting messages that are sent. These might be between the parents: mother might say 'get qualifications'; father might say, 'just get out there and start working – I've achieved plenty without some pointless scrap of paper'. Equally, the contradictions might come from the same parent: she does not practise what she preaches. There can be no certainty about how any one individual might ultimately react to these contradictions. One person might develop a script based on a deep seated unease about what is the right thing to do. Another person might end up with a particularly clear sense of purpose. Somebody else might live their life in a 'mum pleasing' way until the age of thirty five, and then make a dramatic switch to 'please dad'. There is always each person's uniqueness that will come into play, often with some surprising outcomes.

Sometimes scripts can have a particularly daunting coherence to them when it comes to seeking to make changes. However, that very coherence marks its susceptibility to change, since it can be picked apart at any point should somebody want to modify his script. For example, a script with a theme of low self confidence will probably be maintained and reinforced by small daily behaviours; such as always apologising before making a point. This person might start to change his script once aware of it, by stopping the apology and replacing it with, for example, a slightly firmer voice.

It is important to remember there is a great difference between an Adult mediated decision, 'I want to do some things differently from what mum and dad taught me', as opposed to a rebellious (-AC) decision, 'I must prove them wrong at all costs!' The latter is a compulsion which, paradoxically, reinforces the original script. It is also sometimes accompanied by the forlorn but inextinguishable hope that at some point mum and dad will admit to having been wrong. Ultimately, a true 'script release' is mediated by the positive aspects of all the ego states.

A useful refinement to script theory, **mini-scripts** or **drivers**, was developed by Taibi Kahler and Hedges Capers[12]. They identified five very common scripting messages which, they believed, reinforce the major life script. These are: be strong, try hard, hurry up, be perfect, be pleasing. A core driver dynamic is shown below (Fig 17):

Figure 17: An Aspect of Driver Dynamics

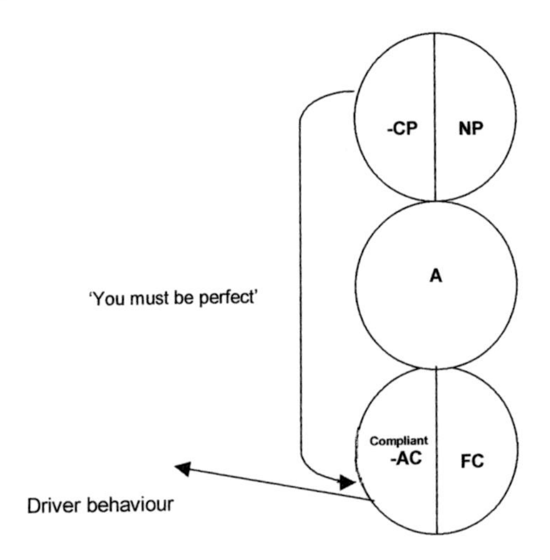

As Capers and Kahler described it, most people have one or two 'favourite' drivers which are essentially habits that the person can fall into very quickly, almost comfortably; typical attitudes and behaviours would then ensue.

Be Perfect. 'I must do everything absolutely perfectly. I set high standards for everything I do. Even if I get 100%, I will think that with more effort I might have got 110%.I tend to enumerate points carefully when I speak, but I can confuse others by trying to cover all points and exceptions, with sub clauses, and then I get so caught up with the accuracy of what I'm trying to say that I forget to pay attention to my audience...just like now.'
Ultimate fear- to be seen as stupid
+ NP Permission needed: to make mistakes.

Be Strong. 'I must not show my feelings, particularly any weakness. One of my favourite sayings is - 'you can't make an omelette without breaking eggs'. I often appear quite stern and indifferent. Sometimes my jaw aches through clenching it so much. On occasion I lapse into a monotone. Often I take on too much, believing I can cope with anything.'
Ultimate fear - to be seen as needy.
+NP Permission needed: to be vulnerable.

Try Hard. 'I firmly believe that nothing comes easily, nor should it do so since life is about struggle. Sometimes you will see me in the 'potty position', straining to make something happen, but to little effect. Often I will start things, but then confuse myself and then have to give up. I labour to understand things, even when simply explained, believing that there must be some hidden complications.'
Ultimate fear – success

+NP Permission needed: to succeed/ to enjoy the moment.

Hurry Up. 'I tend to rush about, arriving early for meetings, impatient that they should start, or late because I fitted another one in at short notice. I can be rather breathless and sweaty, leaping into tasks before I really know what is expected. I'm not a big fan of instruction books. Sometimes I gabble and make everything sound rather urgent.'
Ultimate fear- missing out on something
+NP Permission needed: to take time.

Be Pleasing. 'I like to keep everybody happy. I tend to say yes to things even when I know I can't really do them, and when the requests are contradictory. People tend to ask more and more of me, perhaps it's because I always try to have a smile on my face. Even when people call me whiny, I'm determined still to like them.'
Ultimate fear- being disliked
+NP Permission needed: to please self; not to have to be loved by everyone.

There are a few points of further explanation needed. First, the descriptions above are painted in primary colours. Often driver behaviour is rather more nuanced, even though the underlying motivation might be just as strong.

Secondly, sometimes a person can be 'driven' by two contradictory drivers; for example, be strong and be pleasing. Sometimes this is the result of contradictory messages from the parents. This might lead to some ongoing turmoil – for example, being ruthless and then being desperate to 'kiss and make up'. Alternatively the person might give precedence to one driver for some considerable time, before then switching. All this might, not surprisingly, be confusing for others who, with their anxieties provoked, then switch into *their* driver behaviour.

Thirdly, a person's driver behaviour might only show itself in certain specific areas of his life. For example, somebody might be fairly relaxed about managing staff, but then flip into 'be perfect' whenever it is time for the monthly staff meeting.

Fourthly, driver behaviour can be quite contagious, but getting into the habit of rushing all the time because of having 'a hurry up' boss is not necessarily the same as having a hurry up driver.

Fifthly organisations may implicitly endorse certain types of driver behaviour. One problem with this is that there is always the rebellious 'shadow side' waiting to make its presence felt; for example, the Be Perfect suddenly to make a series of stupid mistakes, the Be Pleasing to be exceptionally rude, the Be Strong to be pathetic, the Hurry Up to be apathetic and the Try Hard to take reckless short cuts.

In all this the presence, or otherwise, of the Adult is vital. There is a world of difference between Be Perfect behaviour and the manager making an Adult decision, 'This report will go before the Board and I want to make it as right as I can'.

Finally, drivers can sometimes explain group behaviour. One department might tend to be rather perfectionist in its approach, and tend to have difficulties with its 'hurry up' neighbours. Under these circumstances collaboration can be tricky, especially if the facilitator brought in to teambuild is into ' be pleasing'.

We now move on to consider some particular applications of TA in organisations.

APPLYING TA IN ORGANISATIONS

Introductory Comments

Since TA provides a theory of personality, behaviour and communication, it offers insight into the dynamics of intrapersonal, interpersonal, group and organisational mind-sets and patterns of relating. So, in terms of management development 'topics', it can contribute to personal awareness, consultancy skills, customer care, conflict management, team building, inter-team building (perhaps as a result of a merger) leadership and organisational culture and change. Regarding this last point, culture change can be seen as script change. It is also excellent for training trainers and facilitators.

It has a wide range of linked models which can be offered with varying levels of complexity. For example, a simple introduction to ego states, strokes and transactions can provide the basis for a two hour session on handling difficult customers. A more complex application could be in using script analysis to help a leadership team examine its past, present and desired future.

TA can generally be seen as an empowering model, emphasising choice, change and responsibility. As such, it is likely to match the values of many training and development organisations, whether internal or external. In many instances the broad pattern in applying TA as a 'helper', whether it be in coaching, training, facilitation, counselling or therapy will be:

Raising client awareness; this awareness being *internal* 'what are my thoughts, feelings and beliefs?' and *external*, 'what do I notice going on around me?'

Helping the client identify choices; that will often mean encouraging the client to question assumptions about which actions might be possible or appropriate.

Supporting the client's experimentation; being available to help the client look at the consequences of new actions and to learn from them.

Establishing clear decisions; helping the client move forward with commitment.

TA's very versatility means that risk needs to be carefully assessed and managed in terms of the content and design of any intervention. To take an extreme example, it would be unwise, and probably unethical, to ask participants on that two hour customer care course to start reflecting on their early childhood experiences. In that setting the trainer would probably be more effective if he concentrates on engaging the trainees' Adult and sense of fun (FC).

From this it is a short step to accepting that the trainer or consultant should have a pretty good understanding of herself in TA terms. So, the need for training and supervision is as relevant here as for any 'helping' specialism.

The basic theory has a high face validity which often means that the client, whether, coachee, trainee or manager can start using the language quite quickly to observe and make comments. As with other models this can lead to an excess of labelling 'You're always using your Critical Parent with me' or an avoidance of personal responsibility 'My life would be so much easier if my parents hadn't given me such a big Adapted Child.' Incidentally, the latter is an example of the game Wooden Leg, a well rehearsed excuse for being a 'failure'.
However, this accessibility can be seen as honouring Berne's legacy of avoiding getting trapped in the mystique of the expert. Of course, participants may well, under these circumstances, make mistakes. What is more important, however, is the process; that people feel free to put forward their views which can then be debated. It is not a matter of the 'helper' denying her own expertise, but rather using it lightly and in an empowering way.

The material lends itself readily to the more traditional development activities such as role plays and observation frameworks. Here it can provide an elegant and simple link between internal processes and external behaviour. In other words, what somebody is saying about herself and others in her head, and what that then leads to in terms of actual communication, both verbal and non verbal. The model clearly offers other options in terms of what the person might say to herself (internal dialogue) or to others (transactions and/or strokes).

It can also be used for 'here and now' interventions, commenting on communication as it happens: 'As you are speaking now my impression is that you are firmly in your Adult. That may not be helpful if you want to motivate people.'

This section is concluded by looking at 'resistance to change'. Clearly this is relevant to any of the 'helper roles' and TA has some interesting perspectives on this.

There is first the fundamental point that resistance to change is not necessarily a 'bad thing'; not all change is, by definition, helpful and productive. Positive resistance to change may come from positive aspects of any of the ego states. For example, "This is contrary to our values" (P); "this is illogical" (A); "this is fishy" (C).

Secondly, resistance to change is often driven by the Child even though the manifestations may be Parent, 'this is outrageous!', or even eminently sensible Adult, 'Can you give me further examples of exactly what this change will specifically mean?' In this latter instance, forensic questioning by the client towards the consultant may be rather more a manifestation of defensiveness (-AC), than a thirst for knowledge. What may well be at stake here are 'survival decisions.' This perhaps sounds a little dramatic but it means, for example, that at some time the boy will have been making decisions on the basis of 'what do I need to do in order to survive and be OK here?' For example, it could be that his decision was to 'keep his head down'.

Years later, a management reorganisation might require that man to be much more prominent, perhaps moving from a back room technical role into a people management function. Under these circumstances it would be surprising if none of those childhood fears re-emerged.

So the consultant, as an agent of change, will need to find ways of engaging the client's Child. There are many options for doing this both direct and indirect. These might include direct feedback, the helper using his Adult to report his own Child feelings, 'I notice that you always want more information and I'm feeling uneasy because ...'; stroking the resistance, perhaps using positive Nurturing Parent and positive Adult, 'Your concern about the change is perfectly understandable, please tell me more...' or choosing to ignore it at that time, but with a view to raising it later. This is an Adult mediated strategic retreat to avoid a possibly unproductive fight.

Also relevant here is the concept of **redefinitions**. That is to say clients, as all of us, will have a particular way of looking at the world, a frame of reference. Sometimes people want to insulate it from reality and will redefine questions which are posed about it. This can be done in either of two ways. One is **tangentially**, where the respondent slightly shifts focus. For example:

Helper: 'Are you willing to support you boss in introducing performance management?'
Client: 'I think it's simply a question of finding a time in the future when I'll be able to do that.'

Here the client retains the topic, but switches from the present to the future.

The other way of redefining is through **blocking**. For example:

Helper: 'Are you willing to support your boss in introducing performance management?'
Client: 'I think that sorting out the bonus system's much more pressing.'

Here the topic is switched.

So the helper will need to be alert to such redefinitions, perhaps consoled by the thought that it is probably a sign that a good and relevant question has been asked, otherwise the client would not feel the need to avoid answering it.

Redefinitions are usually fuelled by the energy of the negative Adapted Child, even though the behaviour manifested may be from other ego states. An example might be the manager who starts patronising a colleague when the latter starts asking highly relevant questions about an ill-conceived project plan.

A point which is perhaps particularly relevant for consultants, since counsellors and therapists may already be aware of it, is the notion of the **gallows transaction**. This was described by Claude Steiner in his work with alcoholics[13]. Regularly somebody would come to support group and say, with a rueful smile and a chuckle, 'I really got drunk last night.' Others would reply with a similar smile and chuckle. This can also happen in business settings. For example, a manager might laugh about being totally unprepared for a performance review and expect a nearby peer to find it equally amusing. In both these instances the attempt is to create a negative Adapted Child to negative Adapted Child transaction (Fig 18) :

Figure 18: A Gallows Transaction

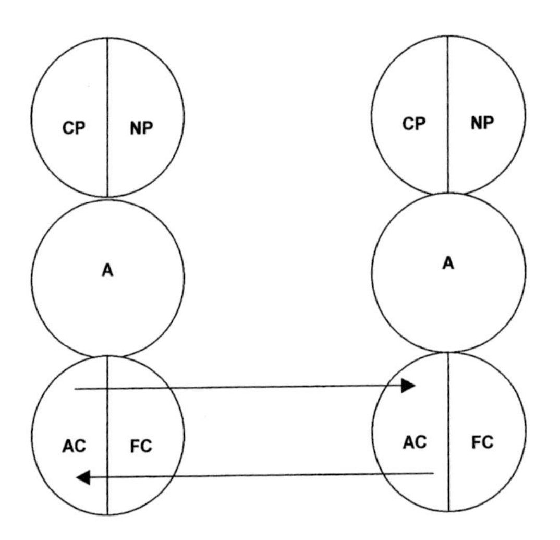

The person is looking to get approval for being self destructive, or incompetent or stupid. If the consultant laughs then he is implicitly endorsing that behaviour. It may be that to some this concern sounds like taking the world too seriously. Although the behaviours may be superficially similar, there is a massive difference between genuine Free Child humour and the unhelpful laughter described above. The reader is invited to use his or her Little Professor to notice the distinction.

The gallows transaction is one of the many behaviours, including drivers and games, which indicate that discounting is taking place. **Discounting** occurs when somebody ignores or minimises some aspect of self, others or the situation which is relevant to solving a problem. Following one of the examples above, the manager minimises her ability to plan properly for a performance review. TA identifies different intensities of discounting. These have been extensively described by Ken Mellor and Eric Sigmund[14]. The diagram below reworks just one small aspect of their thinking (Fig 19).

Figure 19: An Aspect of Discounting

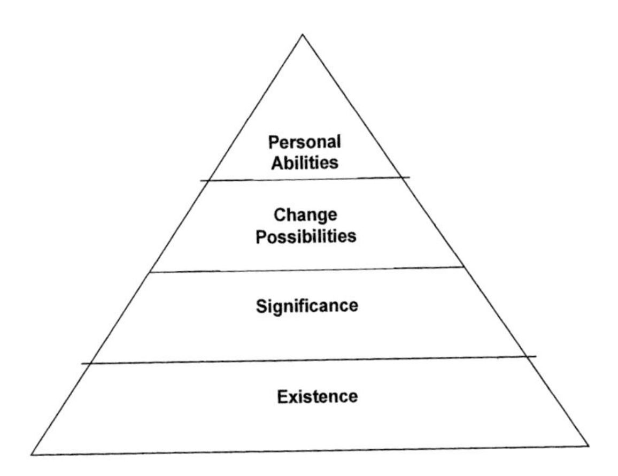

To illustrate the model and the levels, let us assume that an organisation has undergone a massive reorganisation which has been disastrous and led to a 25% drop in revenue.

Existence – this most profound form of discounting. Denying the existence of the problem. The manager here might say, 'We've reorganised a bit, but essentially everything is the same.'

Significance – this is slightly less intense. Minimising the significance of the problem. The manager might say, 'We've had some minor problems as a result of the reorganisation, and this has led to something of a drop in revenue.'

Change possibilities – this is less intense again, since there is recognition of a problem and its scale. However, there is an assumption that nothing can be done about it. The manager might say, 'We've got some major financial problems as a result of the reorganisation, but the revenue decline is so dramatic nobody can do anything about it.'

Personal abilities – this is less intense again, since the scale of the problem, its impact, and the possibilities of changing it are accepted, but the person discounting does not accept that she can personally make a difference. So the manager might say, 'We've got a major problem, but it needs others to sort it out because at my level there is absolutely nothing I can contribute.'

It is vital that the consultant identifies the level of the discounting since that is where the intervention needs to be. If the manager denies the existence of a problem in the first place then there is no point trying to help him or her identify possible actions. The consultant might also find that discounting, perhaps linked to particular business issues, characterises certain teams or relationships; for example, that a group refuses to give feedback to senior management on its change plans because of a collective sense of powerlessness. 'What's the point? .... They can't ..... We won't .... It's too late ....' If, of course, these points are firmly grounded in Adult reality then that is a totally different story.

We will now move on to consider some specific applications of TA in organisations.

TA And Coaching.

This section defines coaching and describes some of the relevant themes, offering some TA perspectives.

First to define some terms, including the often associated helper roles of trainer and counsellor.

Training : a series of managed activities involving individuals and/or groups where a trainer seeks to help a trainee or trainees meet pre-determined objectives.

Counselling : a series of conversations between two individuals where one, the counsellor, seeks to help the other, the client, become more effective in handling personal and life concerns.

Coaching : a series of conversations, usually between two individuals, where one, the coach, seeks to help the other, the coachee, become more effective at work.

There are many different types of coaching, but generally they can be defined as focussing on 'skills', 'performance' or 'life'.

Skills coaching takes a narrow focus on the acquisition of specific task related knowledge and skills; for example, making effective presentations, handling difficult customers or interpreting financial data.

Performance coaching looks wider at the coachee's role and the factors affecting how she carries it out; for example leadership style, self confidence, and risk taking.

Life coaching goes more broadly again and considers the whole person, including home life and long term aspirations.

Obviously these types of coaching are not mutually exclusive, but they point to where the coaching emphasis might be. Indeed they could perhaps be placed on a spectrum of helper roles[15] as shown below (Fig 20).

Figure 20: Helper Roles

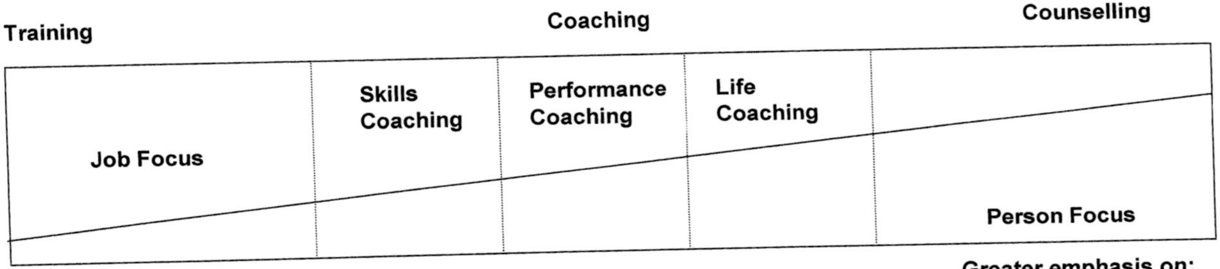

Training	Coaching			Counselling
Job Focus	Skills Coaching	Performance Coaching	Life Coaching	Person Focus

Greater emphasis on:		Greater emphasis on:
Skills	<------------------------------>	Feelings
Job requirements	<------------------------------>	Client requirements
Current and future performance	<------------------------------>	Personal history
Problem solving	<------------------------------>	Personal insight
Client's professional relationships – boss/ colleagues/customers/ staff	<------------------------------>	Client's personal relationships - family/social
Trainer assessing client's progress	<------------------------------>	Counsellor helping client assess own progress

Prompted by this model several themes are considered.

Risk

When moving through skills, performance to life coaching then the risk level may well increase. i.e. the Child ego state feels more vulnerable. Personal history is more legitimately, perhaps inevitably, a likely part of the content, but there is the increased possibility that the coachee may be reaching the limits of self-support.

The higher the risk, the 'stronger', that is to say the more powerful, the Parent ego state of the coach will need to be in offering 'permission' (+NP) and 'protection'(+CP)[16]. There is a greater likelihood that the coach will be encouraging the coachee to question some fundamental beliefs; inevitably many of these beliefs will originate from childhood experiences. So, in some ways even though it is not a therapy relationship, the coach may become an additional or replacement parent (and Parent) figure. It therefore becomes increasingly important that the coach finds ways of 'holding' the coachee. That is to say that the coach will need to be particularly rigorous in setting boundaries, allowing for the fact that a greater intensity of feelings may ensue. These boundaries might relate to topics such as availability, the particular focus of the work and additional specialist help.

This reinforces the fact that the coach needs to offer herself permission and protection. That is, an internal dialogue based upon the positive Nurturing permission (+NP, giving support and encouragement to explore) and Critical Parent protection (+CP, setting limits for safety) in order to be able to offer such qualities to her coachee. If, for example, the coach does not look after herself by keeping her work load manageable, then she will not be able to care for her coachee appropriately.

Success

Successful coaching engages the coachee's Parent, Adult and Child ego states:

Parent - this accords with my values
Adult - this makes sense to me
Child - I'm excited at the prospect

All three need to be present for true commitment.

However, it is important to remember this level of integration by the coachee may only emerge over time. So for example, the coach may, at the beginning, be more effective if he accepts the coachee taking some actions on the basis of compliance (Adapted Child), rather than commitment. This may be a necessary part of the weaning process; an example of positive symbiosis. Of course, if the compliance persists over time then it will become counter-productive, quite possibly indicating that Drama Triangle roles are being played out.

Acting within a script can feel positive through its familiarity, even if it is ultimately unhelpful, or even destructive. This can obviously be as true for the coach as the coachee. It is therefore possible for the coach on occasion to feel that she is being successful when in fact she is supporting the coachee in staying stuck. Two ways of reducing the chances of this happening are first to keep a reflective diary and secondly to receive regular supervision. These activities can help ensure the presence of a compassionate Adult perspective and a heightened alertness to possible collusion between the coach and coachee. Incidentally, as is probably already apparent, TA has many delightful ways of describing collusion: symbiosis, Drama Triangle, games and life positions.

Awareness

There are two interwoven themes to be considered here. One is awareness of the *process* in the relationship. That is to say, the coach using his observation skills and self knowledge to notice what is happening as the coaching unfolds. A traditional short hand way of describing this is being 'a part of, yet apart from' the client; to be sufficiently involved to be fully engaged, yet sufficiently detached to retain perspective.

The other aspect is awareness of the '*technologies*' which are available to support a healthy and productive process. These themes are followed below.

As already mentioned, scripting suggests that people make decisions about the type of people they are, the type of life they will lead, and how they will end up. The earlier in life the decision, the more deeply it is embedded, sometimes being pre-verbal. Therefore some aspects will be less accessible to the coach, and indeed the coachee, and less susceptible to intervention by the coach when using one of his favoured tools......words. So, there is a strong case to be made for the use of non verbal techniques such as pictures, clay modelling, collages, physical movement. These can be helpful in accessing the Child ego state, which is where the most significant script decisions are lodged.
However, as mentioned in the previous section, increased awareness can bring increased risk. Primitive Child ego state issues can be disconcerting, scary and delightful in their simplicity - love, acceptance, existence and nourishment. One way of offering the coachee sufficient safety is to ensure that there are frequent invitations to use the Adult. Some of the options are for the coach to:

- make regular use of the flip chart.
- invite the coachee to use the flip chart.
- ask the coachee to look for themes in the images she has created. In other words to conceptualise.
- to make a theoretical point. If TA is being used as an explicit model then there is certainly plenty of theory from which to choose.
- have a clearly identified Adult chair. This idea originated with psychodrama, but was then extensively used in gestalt (see

later). The coachee has several chairs from which to explore the issue with which she is concerned. The chairs might represent various stakeholders, 'go into the chair representing your boss and see what she might say'; or the chairs might represent the some of the coachee's sub personalities, ego states being an obvious example.

- ask the coachee to use her Adult to report on what her Parent and Child are saying or feeling. This is very different in nature from an invitation directly to express the Parent or Child.

Inevitably, in all this there is the need for the coach to be aware of his own primitive Child ego state and how it might impact on his coaching, whether as support or hindrance. For example, there may be a legacy of a finely tuned sensitivity to unspoken communication, a strong urge to 'be perfect', difficulty in accepting when a coaching relationship is over, or a contagious excitement in learning. Often a coach realises that the question he poses to the coachee is one he could with benefit be asking himself. This carries with it the potential for bringing the coach great clarity, but inevitably there is the possibility of confusion, where for example the coach suggests actions which are much more relevant to himself than the coachee.

Flexibility

The coach needs flexibility in dealing with issues as they arise , yet not lose sight of the points of central concern. As well as this content flexibility the coach's style will also need to be similarly multi-faceted. A TA perspective is to regard this as the ability to move freely between the ego states.

Eric Berne spoke of effective functioning as being dependent upon semi-permeable membranes separating each of the ego states. If there is excessive fluidity (lability) then the coach will probably appear ungrounded; for example, flashes of insight followed by leaps to judgement and neediness. If there is excessive rigidity, for example the failure to use a particular ego state- 'exclusion'- then the coach may, amongst other things, be too much the Mr Spock; the highly analytical Star Trek character. If the coach's ego states overlap ('contamination') then assumption may be presented as fact (P/A), or fantasy as reality (A/C). Such a coach might then have difficulty in helping the coachee clarify and maintain boundaries. Messiness within the coach's internal boundaries will inevitably lead to messiness with external boundaries. This might be shown with such mundane yet vital issues as poor timekeeping or more seriously, game playing. Some would indeed suggest that poor timekeeping is a likely indicator of a game being played. The coachee will intuitively, sometimes with awareness sometimes not, seek partners, such as the coach, to play the complementary hand.

Within the therapy world of TA there is frequent mention of **decontamination**. This means helping the client become clearer about what are fantasies and assumptions, as opposed to reality. The more the ego states overlap, then the greater the contamination. In this setting the contamination, if extreme, might for example include hallucinations or paranoia. Arguably, in a different context and in a much less intense way, coaching is also about decontamination; being alert to, and quite possibly challenging, the client who says, 'I couldn't possibly do that', or 'They would never let me'.

Acknowledgement.

This word is often used in the world of coaching to mean 'offering appreciation'. For example, 'I want to acknowledge your courage in dealing with this issue. The word 'acknowledge' is never used negatively. For example, 'I want to acknowledge your stupidity in failing to face up to this issue'.

In TA the equivalent is about giving positive strokes. Some of the positive strokes that the coach can give are to:

- ensure that the room is comfortable for the coachee; depending on the circumstances that might mean not making it too formal or informal. The use of patchouli, or even lavender, incense sticks for coaching sessions in the executive boardroom is probably a bad idea.
- start the session on time.
- ask for feedback.
- make sure that note taking is not intrusive.

There may be a team dimension here. If the coach works as part of a team then her well being and readiness to give her client positive strokes may be dependent upon the extent to which she receives positive strokes from her colleagues. As a very rough rule of thumb, the more stroke starved the coach is, the more likely that any sort of negative feedback from the coachee will be magnified internally (Fig 21).

Figure 21: Magnifying the Stroke

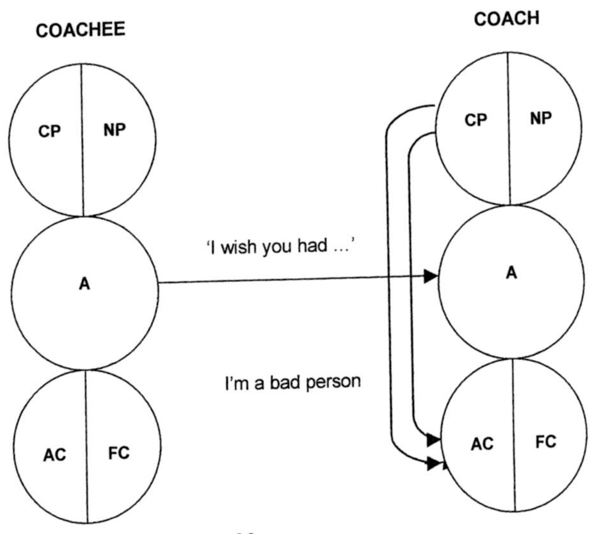

So there is a responsibility, indeed an ethical obligation for the coaching team and its management, to ensure that it operates in a 'healthy' way. As mentioned in the next section, TA can be used for team building. This is obviously as true for teams of coaches as teams of managers. It may be that internal coaching teams need to be particularly alert to the TA patterns they have in common with their client organisation. There will certainly be quite a lot in common, otherwise they would not be able to co-exist. The skill is in recognising where those similarities are a little too great, blunting their capacity to be agents of change.

Whether being an internal or external coach sensitivity to the organisational context within which the coachee operates is clearly vital.

TA can, as mentioned earlier, provide a link between individual behaviour and organisational culture. So, for example, the coachee may tend to over-intellectualise and problem solve solely through clinical detachment; excessive use of the Adult ego state. This may parallel the way in which the coachee's organisation is led and a prevailing currency of cleverness. In supporting the coachee in making changes the coach will need to be aware of the powerful Parent which may police and reward such behaviour. The coach may be in the position of supporting the coachee in making changes which go against the prevailing culture. Faced with this it will be important for the coach to revisit the contract regularly; perhaps, with the agreement of the coachee, involving the sponsor.

Sometimes people join an organisation in order to perpetuate the family script. So along with the Parent figures of the organisation there might also be other 'presences' who are equally important, namely those Parent figures who helped create the coachee's script in the first place. So the coach would do well to be alert to any 'adverse reaction' after a script breaking change by the coachee. This adverse reaction could be a **rubberband**[17], which means suddenly going back in time and re-experiencing the feelings associated with the original script decision. It might not always be intense but could be, for example, some low level guilt or sadness for having now broken one of mum or dad's rules. This can still happen as a grown up when, even with supreme Adult clarity, one can see the unhelpful or even toxic quality in the original message. There may be quite an emotional reaction simply because of the realisation that one new behaviour did not have a particularly significant impact, despite the effort entailed.

In all this, the coach may find it helpful to maintain the best practice routine of:

Ensuring that any behaviour stopped by the client has a clear replacement. This reduces the chances of the coachee feeling 'scriptless'; that is being in an anonymous or even existential void.

Clearly and directly 'stroking' the new behaviour, even if the behaviour was not totally 'successful'.

Using the sort of strokes that will be most valued by the coachee; perhaps for ingenuity in trying something new; or, tenacity in having persisted; or wisdom in knowing when to pull back.

Encouraging the coachee to find ways of rewarding himself whether, for example, tangibly or a moment's quiet reflection.

Helping the coachee establish other sources of support; rather as if helping the coachee to establish an alternative or additional family.

The benefits of keeping a diary have already been mentioned. However, to conclude with an additional point here. TA can usefully support this 'reflective practice' by providing a framework: reflecting on stroking patterns with the coachee, dominance of ego states, possible symbiosis whether positive or negative, use of feelings and rackets and the impact of scripts. This can then become a useful language for peer supervision.

TA And Teambuilding

Just as coaching has many manifestations, so does team building. Some will think of a team in crisis, needing to go off-site for a couple of days to 'sort things out'. Others will think of a more routine form of housekeeping where, as part of its monthly meeting, the team carries out a process review- 'how well are we working with each other ?' Equally some might think of externally facilitated events, perhaps with an outward bound component, others might think of events which are not facilitated at all. Again others might think of an agenda which is fairly open, the content being decided at the time, or one which has a strong business focus, or a softer, looser agenda based on people 'getting to know each other better'.
With this rich mixture of possibilities the reader is asked to modify or discard any subsequent points which may not fit in to the particular type of team building he or she has in mind.
Below, adapted from original work by John Adams and Sabina Spencer, (Fig 22) is offered a very broad overview of team building, suggesting that it can be fitted into any one of four domains. Each box gives an example.

Figure 22: Domains of Teambuilding

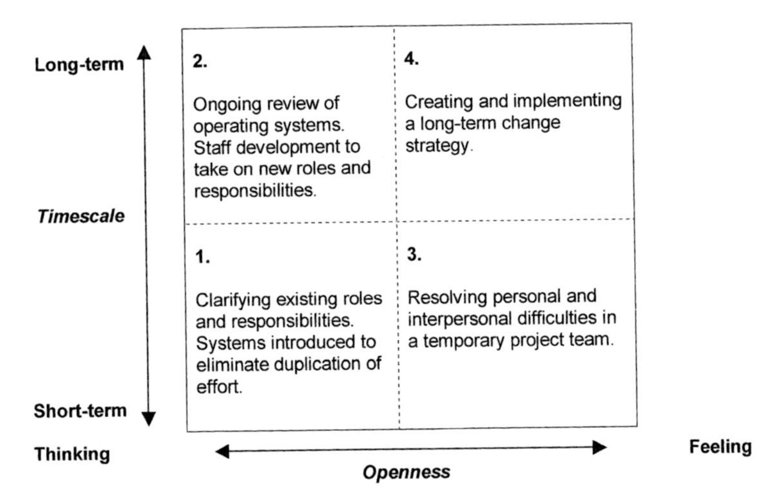

Domain one is largely concerned with short term, 'technical' problem solving.

Domain two is concerned with longer term, technical planning, anticipating future problems.

Domain three is concerned with short term, 'relationships' problem solving.

Domain four is concerned with longer term vision creation and is likely to involve some technical and relationships issues.

The dotted lines indicate that the domains are not mutually exclusive. For example, a leadership team might decide that it needs to spend time on long term vision creation, but then discover that there are some urgent interpersonal difficulties that need to be addressed. Or a team working on longer term technical communication issues then realises that it needs more clarity on its vision. However, the model is designed simply to show a point of emphasis that may then change.

Against this backdrop TA can be used as an *implicit* model to focus the team, engaging with Parent, Adult and Child themes. It is important to remember that the involvement of all the positive ego states is as important for group, as individual development.

At a *content* level this might mean:

Parent – What traditions are to be maintained? Which ones discarded? What values do we hold dear? How do we build/maintain support for our customers, staff, ourselves? What non negotiable demands do we want to place on ourselves/others?

Adult – What is the 'Martian' view of our business. What are its assets and liabilities? What would our best friend and worst critic say? What are the grains or boulders of truth in what they say?

Child – What excites us at present? What are we fearful of? How can we build/ maintain freshness and creativity?

At a *process* level this might mean the team builder seeking to engage the Parent, Adult and Child aspects of the team. For example:

Parent – Invitations to be open about important personal beliefs about business; creating a safe environment where people can exchange feedback. Encouragement to offer and be willing to model challenge and support. A willingness to challenge phoney questions; that is, questions which mask a statement.

Adult – Offering a rich array of analytical problem solving techniques. Ensuring that the question, 'what's the contrary view?', is always posed. Maintaining reasonably open (semi permeable) boundaries so that, for example suppliers and customers have a respected contribution. This reduces the chances of 'group think', which is negative Adapted Child phenomenon.

Child - Providing plenty of opportunities for creativity and excitement. For example, imagery, pictures, using analogies, story telling and role plays. Of course these need to be matched to the culture, but not too much. If the team has a deep loathing for role plays then introducing them will probably elicit negative Critical Parent or negative Adapted Child reactions.

On occasion the team builder might use TA *explicitly* considering such questions as:

What sort of strokes/recognition do you typically give each other?

What is your script in terms of - seeing yourselves as a family – who is the earth mother, the wicked step mother, big daddy, the black sheep?

- seeing yourselves as a sport or soap opera? Who plays what roles? Is there another sport which would better represent what you want to be? How could you bring that closer to reality?

What stamp collections have you brought? What stamp collections do you imagine each of you brings?

Role plays to experiment with using different ego states. Perhaps recording on CCTV and using TA to review the results.

Completing some TA -based self assessment questionnaires[18] and comparing the results.

Holding a normal business meeting, then using TA as the basis for the review.

All of these points apply equally to inter-team building. Where, for example, there are mergers and acquisitions then different scripts come together; there are then decisions to be made about what is to be retained, developed or discarded. The challenge is about being open to possibilities, but this at a time when fear and paranoia may be at its most heightened. TA, whether used explicitly or implicitly, can provide a framework for exploring some of the key issues.

In summary it is about using TA sensitively bearing in mind the prevailing culture, knowing when to accommodate it and when to challenge. Essentially, as indicated in the model below (Fig 23), managing the risk level with a view to maximising the willingness to learn.

Figure 23: The Energy of Learning

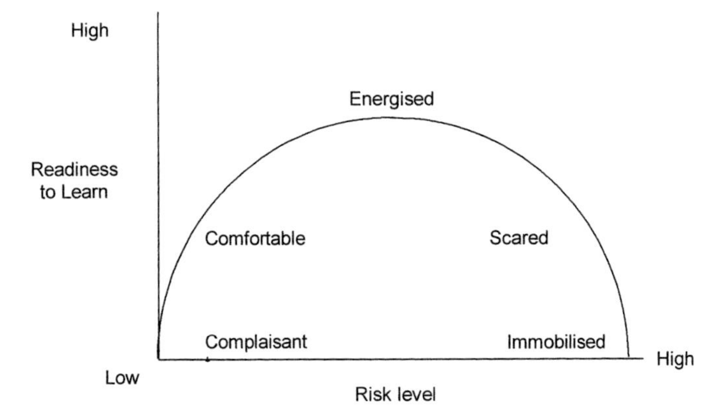

TA and FIRO-B

The Fundamental Interpersonal Relations Orientation –Behaviour model was developed by Will Schutz[19]. It can provide some valuable insights into personal and interpersonal style. It has many business applications, including the exploration of team patterns for those who are managed at a distance. The basic model assumes that when people come together there are likely to be three sets of needs: for *inclusion*, that is to belong and associate; for *control*, that is to be able to influence; and for *affection*, that is to get emotionally close to others. These needs will vary for each person in two areas. First there is importance; for example, control is more significant for some people than others. Secondly people may vary in the extent to which they initiate and *express* the need or the extent to which they *want* others to show inclusion, control or affection behaviours towards them. The FIRO-B instrument, therefore, gives the person some information about their behaviour in six areas: Expressed Inclusion, Wanted Inclusion, Expressed Control, Wanted Control, Expressed Affection and Wanted Affection.

It is possible to add to a FIRO-B by speculating on some TA perspectives:

Whether the person tends to use a particular ego state for any of their Inclusion, Control and Affection behaviours. For example, there will be a qualitative difference between Expressed Control having Adult, as opposed to Critical Parent, energy behind it.

Within a TA frame of reference every behaviour is regarded as ultimately having a Child need behind it. Perhaps an additional TA perspective with FIRO-B would be to help the client explore whether his core motivation, either generally or on a particular issue, is motivated by Inclusion, Control or Affection needs. The words themselves indicate core 'survival' needs, decided at an early age in order to be OK. Almost by definition, FIRO-B patterns will be based on script decisions.

There will probably be certain stroking patterns (whether internal or external) related to Inclusion, Control and Affection behaviours. For example, a person may give others lots of positive strokes in support of her Expressed Inclusion behaviour; equally, Wanted Affection behaviours may be accompanied by giving self negative strokes.

TA may be helpful in examining with a client mismatches between behaviour and intention. For example, using Critical Parent energy in when Expressing Inclusion may be counterproductive, particularly if the person's Free Child is anxiously present in Wanted Affection.

Transactions and symbiosis can be used to look at FIRO-B patterns of communication. For example, somebody using Critical Parent energy in Expressed Control getting into unhelpful patterns of communication with somebody who has Adapted Child energy in their Wanted Control.

The idea of ulterior transactions may help the client explore the extent to which, for example, she presents to the world an Expressed Affection personality (social level), whilst behind it there is a strong Expressed Control need (psychological level).

A further refinement of these levels of communication is to speculate whether it is possible to identify social, psychological and existential levels, perhaps based on the FIRO-B needs. For example (Fig 24), that generally a person leads with Control,(social), that behind this there is Affection, (psychological), but that at core the person's concern is Inclusion, (existential).

Figure 24: Combined Levels of Communication

Surface Level

Social **Control**

Persecutor

Psychological **Rescuer** **Affection**

Victim

Existential **Inclusion**

Deep Level

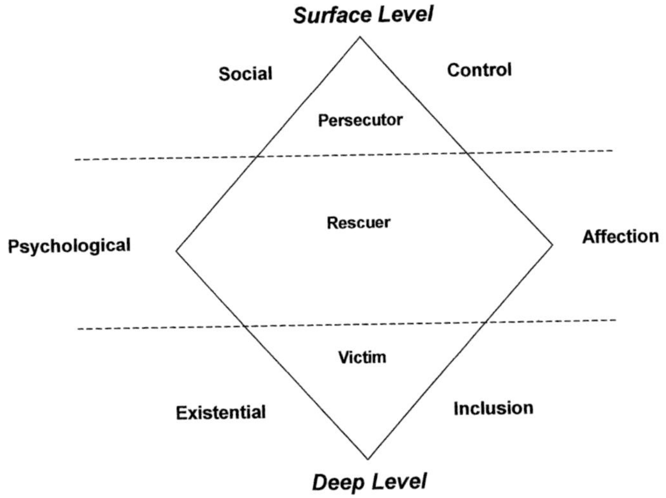

This builds on Graham Barnes'[20] idea that similar distinctions could be made with the Drama Triangle positions; for example, the person presents Persecutor to the world, this masks Rescuer and at the core is Victim.

Both TA and FIRO-B use simple and accessible language. This can risk oversimplification, but this potential difficulty can be more than outweighed by the advantages of clarity and impact.

TA and Assertiveness Training.

TA lends itself well to this for reasons which have been covered elsewhere: it links the internal and the external, it identifies clear options and it can link the past with the present.

One aspect of TA theory which can be useful here is drawn from, and heavily adapts, (Fig 25) **The Racket System** developed by Richard Erskine and Marilyn Zalcman[21].

Unassertive behaviour, whether passive, aggressive or passively hostile, is likely to be the result of an integrated and self contained pattern of:

Beliefs	about self, others and the world (For example, 'I never get what I really want')
Behaviours	acting on those beliefs and 'inviting' the reinforcing behaviour from others. (For example, not expressing wants clearly and consequently not being listened to.)
	physical symptoms (For example, stooping a little, perhaps some back pain)
Feelings	at this time feeling, for example, guilty or inadequate
Reinforcing memories	having a number of memories, which have now just been added to, of occasions in the recent or distant past of being somebody who never gets what she really wants. This then reinforces the Belief.

Figure 25: Modified Racket Systems

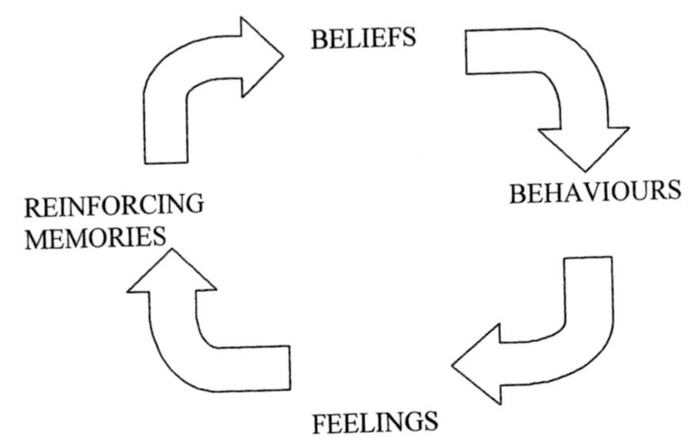

It is a vicious, self reinforcing cycle. However, this means that it can be broken at any point as a means of turning this non assertive cycle into an assertive one.

The first stage is to help the person identify the more detailed content of their non assertive pattern. This works best if this exploration centres around one particular incident.

For a lot of people, behaviours will be a good entry point. Below are some illustrative questions and suggestions to consider.

Allow the client some time to gather her thoughts about a recent event when she was not as assertive as she would have wished. Give her time to identify some aspects of the context, the lead up to the event, the location, perhaps some of the sights and sounds. Then narrow the focus, using the cycle as a guide.

Behaviours : What do you recall as your behaviours at the time ? How do you think you might have looked to a disinterested observer? Do you recall your posture? What words do you recall of yours and the other people involved?

Feelings : What feelings did you have ? Did you have different intensities of feelings? Did they change during this episode? If so, how?

Memories : In reflecting on the above do you have any sense of déjà vu? In other words, have you been in similar situations in the past? What examples do you recall?

Beliefs : In reflecting on these situations do you believe they say something about the type of person you are ? What does it say about the other people?

It is important to allow for some guesses and speculations, or even some blanks since the person may not be clear about all aspects. The aim then is to begin to put in place the components which will begin to turn it into a virtuous, assertive cycle. People will vary in terms of their preferred entry point for doing this. Some will for example find it easier to think of some positive memories, others might be much more aware of their body and behaviours.

It is then a matter of practising and experimenting with some of these new insights and understandings, gradually filling in and refining the components of the assertive pattern.

Incidentally, assertiveness is about using all the positive aspects of all the ego states, not just Adult. So for example, there is a world of difference between assertive anger (+ CP), which is focussed and specific, and aggressive anger (- CP) which is expressed as an end in itself, without purpose. It is similar to the difference made in psychosynthesis between being any angry person as opposed to being somebody who chooses on occasion to be angry[22].

Often it is worth being alert to the person's sighs as she is helped to explore and complete the cycle. As Lawrence Collinson explained in a supervision workshop, a sigh usually indicates a change of ego state. So a sigh may indicate that the client has slipped from Adult to Adapted Child; that at the point of change the 'old' self regains prominence.

Transactional Analysis and Gestalt.

It has long been recognised that gestalt and TA complement each other very well. For example, a book which made a major contribution to popularising TA was 'Born to Win – Transactional Analysis with Gestalt Experiments', by Muriel James and Dorothy Jongeward, first published in 1971.

What follows is not intended to be a detailed exposition of gestalt, but rather sufficient explanation briefly to indicate some of the links with TA. Gestalt psychology originated in Germany in the 19th century. One of the key observations of the 'gestalt' school was that human beings have a drive for completeness; to make things whole, to complete the gestalt. That is, people create patterns in order to make sense of their experience and to avoid 'unfinished business.' One of the most frequently used examples to illustrate this point is to 'see' the dots below as a circle.

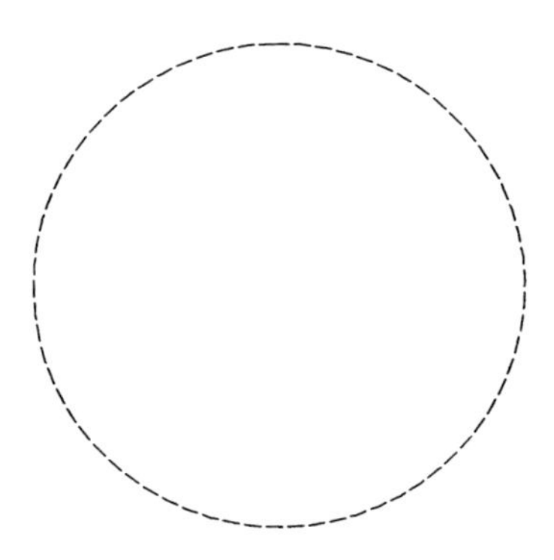

In other words, in our mind's eye we will tend to fill in the gaps between the dots in order to be able to call it a circle. Fritz Perls (1893-1970), developed gestalt thinking into an approach to psychotherapy[23], exploring the ways in which people can support or block themselves in dealing with 'unfinished business'. For example, if somebody feels very irritated with a colleague coming late to a vital meeting, but says nothing about it, then there is unfinished business; it takes energy to block energy and to carry on as if nothing had happened; that energy is not then available to deal with the next event, whatever that might be. The irritated manager may then, in order to deal with his own discomfort and 'complete the circle', imagine all sorts of excuses for his colleague; this would be a way of explaining to himself not only his colleague's behaviour, but also his own - his failure to question or confront.

As Richard Erskine put it in a conference presentation[24], a script decision is a way of contriving a completion of something that would not otherwise make sense. He illustrated it as below (Fig 26):

Figure 26: Scripts and Gestalt Completion

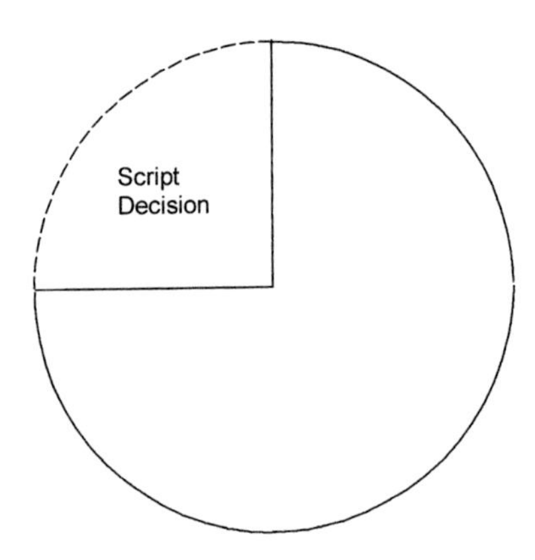

To take a rather more dramatic example: a clever child is faced with the painful fact that her parents frequently adversely compare her to her elder brother. She may decide, 'I must be stupid', in order to deal with the tensions and contradictions in the situation. Again, Perls would regard such a decision as a cause of unfinished business, even if the habit of 'acting stupid' became deeply ingrained and the girl became a woman who truly believed it.

He saw 'awareness' of wants, needs and feelings as crucial in dealing with the unhelpful legacies of the past. In doing so he with other Gestalt therapists identified a number of common blocks to awareness, each of which can be interpreted through TA.

Confluence. That is over identifying with another person, 'your pain is my pain'. Such merged boundaries could be illustrated as follows (Fig 27):

Figure 27: Ego States and Confluence

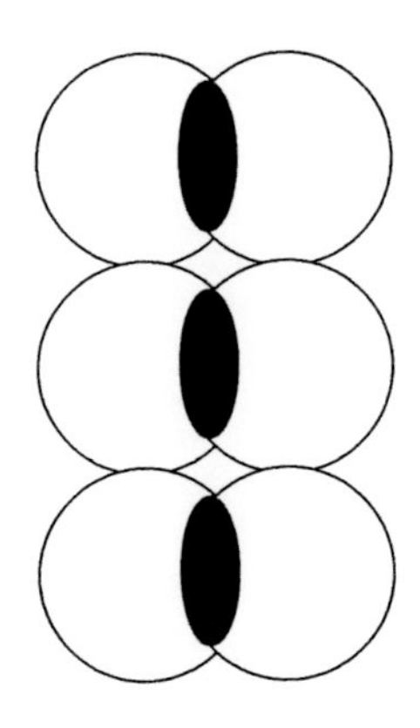

Introjection. That is, the swallowing whole of a rule; not chewing it to decide which parts to digest and which parts to discard. It is a lodged in the Adapted Child. The unthinking habits which then ensue may be harmless. For example, Berne tells the story of a woman who always cut the end off a leg of ham before boiling it. When her daughter asked her about it, pointing out that the saucepan was in fact big enough to contain it whole, the woman did not know why. In time they discovered that when she herself was a girl then her mother did not have a big enough saucepan so the ham had to be cut in order for it to be cooked. However other introjects might be more harmful; for example, 'I must shout to get listened to'.

Projection. That is about attributing to others qualities that one does not acknowledge in oneself. For example, the Rescuer denies her own neediness and will attribute to others, the Victims, a neediness which may well not be there, but which the Rescuer needs to 'see' in order to make sense of her own role.

Retroflection. That is about doing to oneself what one wants to do to somebody else. For example, turning one's anger inwards, and giving oneself a negative stroke, rather than giving the negative stroke to the person who 'deserved' it, perhaps then getting a migraine.

Deflection. That is turning the other person aside. This might be done directly, for example by doodling and totally ignoring what is said; or indirectly by, for example, arguing over definitions. 'Do you value my contribution to the team?' 'It depends what you mean by value'. These are very similar to the TA idea of redefinitions (see above).

Perls also saw it as important that people develop an awareness of their 'shoulds' (internal Parent rules leading to Adapted Child behaviour, for example), and 'wants' (Free Child.) Sometimes a 'should' can become so habitual that it almost feels like a want. It has the cosy familiarity of an old overcoat, even though the seams are torn and it lets the rain in.

So, boundary clarification and management are fundamental aims in both TA and gestalt. As such these models can, for example, provide a valuable guide for the organisation development consultant. In his book, 'Organizational Consulting- a Gestalt Approach'[25], Ed Nevis considers the skills needed of a consultant, or 'skilled intervenor'. Much of what he describes could be reinterpreted using the language and philosophy of TA as shown in brackets below. For example, he writes of the need to:

- put things succinctly, clearly and directly;(to avoid getting into driver behaviour)

- separate data from interpretation; (to notice when one is using Parent or Adult in assessing what is emerging from the client organisation)

- accept emotional situations with a minimum of personal defensiveness; (to recognise when racket feelings are being expressed, and not to respond in kind)
- be both tough and supportive during the same work session; (to use positive aspects of all the ego states)
- be able to appreciate the importance of fantasy and imagination;(to allow scope for the use of the Free Child and Little Professor)

Both TA and Gestalt provide a rich spectrum of styles and interventions ranging from the specific detail of personal behaviour to the broad sweep of the moral and strategic approach involved in being a change agent.

Transactional Analysis and Appreciative Inquiry.

Once again the aim here is not to offer a comprehensive description of Appreciative Inquiry (AI), but to consider several of its features through the lens of TA.

When David Cooperrider and Suresh Srivastva began developing their ideas in the 1980's, it was as a reaction against research which, to their mind, was all too often focussed on problems rather than creative possibilities. They believed that from this frame of mind there emerged an impoverished landscape where the emphasis was placed on what has gone wrong rather than what is going well; damage limitation, rather than growth; blame rather than progress; deficits, rather than resources; and perfection, rather than action.

Four of the principles they elucidated to underpin a more optimistic view were:

Appreciation: that is looking for what is working. There is a clear link here with the idea of positive strokes, given to self and others. It is perhaps not surprising that when AI is successfully applied then there is often mention of the great energy and enthusiasm that is released[26]. Clearly this can be in contrast to those situations where an over emphasis on finding the problem and what has gone wrong may lead to a lack of positive strokes, an excess of negative strokes, and the existence of stroke voids, where no strokes of any sort are given. This is very similar to the world of the '**stroke economy**', as described by Claude Steiner[27]:

Don't give strokes when you have them to give
Don't ask for strokes when you need them
Don't accept strokes if you want them
Don't reject strokes when you don't want them
Don't give yourself strokes

In such an environment positive strokes become a precious commodity, instead of a natural part of everyday life. This then has implications for people's feelings of self worth, willingness to take risks, and authenticity.

As described elsewhere, if positive strokes are in short supply then people will do anything to get some form of recognition, even if it is negative. (e.g.games)

Applicability: that is, looking for practical applications. Encouraging people to use their Adult and creative Child.

Provocation: that is, looking for ways to challenge assumptions and evoke what might be. This in an invitation to revisit Parental rules and the consequential Adapted Child habits - 'we've always done it this way'. New possibilities may well come from permissions to use intuition (Little Professor) and Free Child energy and creativity.

Collaboration: that is, looking for ways to extend dialogue and debate. No group, therefore, is automatically excluded; contaminations, such as 'we know without asking that Department, that they've nothing to contribute', would be challenged. True collaboration would also mean that those involved are encouraged to bring all their talents; namely, the positive aspects of all their ego states. For example, in debating how to move the organisation forward, everybody is allowed, indeed, encouraged, to be the best they are and the best they can be.

AI has an increasingly wide range of application – for example, education, coaching, organisation development, equal opportunities and TA is well positioned to support each of these areas.

Script Exercise.

As previously mentioned risk and the contract need to be given serious consideration in advance. These questions and any subsequent review should not be treated as a 'fill in exercise'. ('We've got a few minutes to spare, might as well ask them to answer the script questions.') The illustration of its use described here assumes a group setting. The questions are equally valid for one to one work.

The questions are likely to vary in their relevancy from one person to another. As a general rule allow each person to choose on which questions he wants to concentrate.

Reviewing and refining the answers in a pair or small group will be a good source of 'protection', as well as the accompanying encouragement to consider the work implications. Of course in some situations, for example counselling or life coaching, the non work aspects may be equally relevant.

1. Write a short pen portrait for each of your 'carers', as you would have seen them at around age eight. For example, their appearance, 'catch phrases', their attitude to you. Please focus on each of them separately, even if they had some things in common.

2. What sorts of things did you get 'rewarded' and 'punished' for, and how?

3. What stories, real or embellished, were told about you?

4. What nickname(s), if any, did you have?

5. If you really wanted to upset them, what did you/might you have done?

6. If you really wanted to please them, what did you/might you have done?

7. Do you recall any particular stories – fact and/or fiction- that had a particular impact on you?

8. Was anybody held up to you as a good or bad example?

9. What rules, if any, did they give you about life? For example, about money, sex, work, relationships? Once again, please distinguish the source if you can.

10. Do you recall any formative events, and any decisions you made linked to those events?

In reflecting on your answers above, are there any aspects which are particularly relevant for how you behave at work now? If it's helpful you might wish to relate it to particular organisational responsibilities. For example, how you lead, delegation style, change management, project management, staff management and development, 'followership' skills, customer care, organisational politics.

Which ones serve you well and you wish to retain?

Which ones might you wish to modify or discard?

Talk your answers through with a colleague here and be ready to mention one point in the group.

BIBLIOGRAPHY

TA Today - A New Introduction to Transactional Analysis. Ian Stewart and Vann Joines. Lifespace. Lifespace Publishing. 1987. An excellent, comprehensive and easily understood presentation to the theory and its applications.

Transactional Analysis for Trainers. Julie Hay. Sherwood. 1996. As well as the theory and practical tips for trainers, it offers plenty of practical exercises.

TA and Training: The Theory and Use of TA in Organisations. Dave Barker. Gower. 1980. Very easy to read and grounded in the practicalities of TA in a training setting. (Second hand only).

Transactional Analysis Counselling in Action. Ian Stewart. Sage. 2002. Another excellent book with a masterly blend of theory and practice.

Scripts People Live. Claude Steiner. Avalon. 2002. Certainly one of the classic texts on scripts and script theory.

Beyond Games and Scripts. Eric Berne. Grove Press.1976.A useful overview, based on extracts from his major writings.

Transactional Analysis – a Relational Perspective. Helena Hargaden and Charlotte Sills. Brunner Routledge.2003. A meticulously researched book written particularly with the therapist reader in mind.

Skills in Transactional Analysis Counselling and Therapy. Christine Lister-Ford. Sage. 2002. A really nice blend of theory, checklists and case studies.

The Transactional Manager. Abe Wagner. Industrial Society. 1996. A personal and accessible look at TA from a management perspective.

FURTHER CONTACTS

The major professional bodies are The Institute for Transactional Analysis, The Institute for Developmental Transactional Analysis, The European Association for Transactional Analysis and the International Transactional Analysis Association. A web search will provide up to date information on the separate and joint conferences that are run, as well as guidance on training (in the fields of organisational applications, education, counselling and psychotherapy), local workshops, articles, ethics, and different categories of membership.

REFERENCES

1. 'I'm OK, You're OK'. Thomas Harris. Grove Press. 1967

2. 'The OK Corral : the grid for get on with'. Franklin Ernst. Transactional Analysis Journal 1. 4. 1971

3. 'Intuition and Ego States'. Eric Berne. TA Press. 1977

4. Hawthorne Experiments : ' Management and Organisation Behaviour'. Laurie Mullins. Pitman. 1993

5. 'Gifts Differing: Understanding Personality Type.' Isabel Briggs Myers. OPP Books. 1980

6. 'Games People Play'. Eric Berne. Penguin. 1964

7. 'Fairy Tales and Script Drama Analysis'. Stephen Karpman. Analysis Bulletin. 7. 26. 1968

8. 'The Gestalt Approach :An Introduction for Managers and Trainers'. Neil Clark and Tony Fraser. Roffey Park Institute. 1982

9. 'The Other Side of Power'. Claude Steiner. Grove Press. 1981

10. 'Emotional Intelligence'. Daniel Goleman. Bantam. 1995

11. An adaptation of the original diagram by Claude Steiner in 'Script and Counterscript'. TA Bulletin. 5. 18. 1966

12. 'The Miniscript' by Taibi Kahler from 'TA After Eric Berne'. Graham Barnes (ed) Harpers College Press 1977

13. 'Games Alcoholics Play'. Claude Steiner. Grove Press 1971

14. 'Cathexis Reader'. Jacqui Lee Schiff. Harper Row 1975

15. 'Coaching in Organisations : Between the Lines'. Keri Phillips Claremont 2004

16. 'Permission and Protection'. Patricia Crossman. Transactional Analysis Bulletin 5 19 1966

17. 'Dictionary of Transactional Analysis'. Tony Tilney. Whurr. 2003

18. For example, Julie Hay has developed questionnaires related to working styles, ego states and life positions.
See www.sherwoodpublishing.com

19. 'FIRO- A Three Dimensional Theory of Interpersonal Behaviour'. Will Shutz. Muir Beach CA Will Schutz Associates 1989

20. 'On Saying Hello: The Script Drama Diamond and Character Role Analysis'. Graham Barnes. Transactional Analysis Journal. January 1981

21. 'The Racket System: A Model for Racket Analysis'. Richard Erskine and Marilyn Zalcman. Transactional Analysis Journal 9. 1. 1979

22. 'What We May Be'. Piero Ferrucci. Turnstone Press 1984

23. 'Gestalt Therapy: Excitement and Growth in the Human'. Frederick Perls, Ralph Hefferline and Paul Goodman. Pelican 1973

24. 'Script Cure: Behavioural, Intrapsychic and Physiological'. Richard Erskine. Transactional Analysis Journal. 1980

25. 'Organisational Consulting – A Gestalt Approach'. Edwin Nevis. Gestalt Institute of Cleveland. 1987

26. 'Appreciative Inquiry'. Jane Magruder Watkins and Bernard Mohr. Jossey Bass 2001

27. 'The Stroke Economy'. Claude Steiner. Transactional Analysis Journal 3. 1971

Other books by this author :

‘Creative Coaching : Doing and Being’. KPA 2007

‘Intuition in Coaching’. KPA 2006

‘Coaching in Organisations : Between the Lines’. Claremont 2004

‘A Consultancy Approach for Trainers and Developers’. Gower. 1997
(with Patricia Shaw)